HIGHLY SENSITIVE

A Beginner's Guide to Learn the Best Techniques and Methods to Thrive as a Highly Sensitive Person

Table of Contents

Chapter 1: What Is a Highly Sensitive Person?..................................... 1

Things You Need to Know About Highly Sensitive People 2

Science-Based Qualities That Characterize
an Exceedingly Sensitive Individual 3

The World Needs More Exceptionally Sensitive Individuals........... 6

We Need Very Sensitive Individuals on the Following Grounds..... 7

Indications of Being a Very Sensitive Individual.............................. 8

Classification One: Affectability about Oneself............................... 9

Classification Two: Affectability about Others............................... 10

Classification Three: Affectability about One's Condition 11

**Chapter 2: Self-Tests to Find out If You Are
a Highly Sensitive Person** 13

Sensation-Seeking Test... 13

Highly Sensitive Child Test.. 15

Am I a Highly Sensitive Person Test 17

Chapter 3: Sensitivity, Your Body, and Your Brain 21

What Makes an HSP's Brain Different?... 22

Having a Highly Sensitive Mind Is a Gift 24

The Reason Behind an HSP Absorbing Other People's Emotions. 25

Prioritizing Your Needs... 26

Why HSPs Need Sound Boundaries.. 28

Chapter 4: What Do Highly Sensitive People Need to Be Happy? .. 30

An HSP Needs to Live a Slow-Paced Life 30

An HSP Needs Time to Rest After a Long Day 31

An HSP Needs a Safe Haven to Relax 31

An HSP Needs to Know It's All Right to Cry and Get Emotional ... 31

An HSP Needs the Time to Absorb Changes 31

An HSP Needs to Make Close, Important Connections 32

An HSP Needs a Solid Method of Handling Conflict 32

An HSP Needs a Decent Night's Rest 33

An HSP Needs to Maintain a Healthy Diet throughout the Day ... 33

An HSP Needs to Have an Outlet for Their Inventive Side 34

An HSP Needs a Solid Feeling of Direction 34

An HSP Needs Friends and Family Who Understand
and Regard Their Sensitive Nature 34

An HSP Needs a Glimpse of Nature Every Now and Then 35

Chapter 5: How to Live with Being a Highly Sensitive Person 36

Stop Hunting Down Somebody or Something to Fix You 38

Let Yourself Know That You Are Not Fake 38

Search for Like-Minded People and Realize That
You are Not the Only One 39

Search for the Concealed Energy in Each Circumstance
and Relish in It 40

Find New Ways to Deal with Old Tricks 41

Treat Yourself with Sympathy 41

Create Boundaries That Aren't Ridden with Emotion 42

Listen to What Your Body Tells You in Order to
Avoid Emotional Strain 43

Make Use of Healthy Habits 43

Don't Try to Suppress Your Sensitivity 44

Chapter 6: How to Live with a Highly Sensitive Person **46**

Talk in a Soft Tone When You Are Near Them 46

Sensitive People Don't Complain as Much as You Might Think.... 47

Sensitive Individuals Are Huge Art Lovers 47

Sensitive Individuals Do Not Like the Feeling of Being Drunk....... 47

Don't Invite a Sensitive Person for a Session at the Gym 48

Allow Sensitive Individuals to Zone Out 48

Let Them Stare into Nothingness 48

Don't Retaliate at Their Criticism 49

It's Normal for Sensitive People to Endure Days
without Human Interaction 49

Be Honest about Your Own Feelings........................... 49

Don't Push Your Political Opinions onto Sensitive Individuals 50

Similar to the Above, Religion Is a Sensitive Subject as Well........ 50

Listening to the Listener 50

Do Not Plan Their Day for Them 51

Don't Think Sensitive People Are Judging 51

Don't Think You Need to Take Them for a Drink to
Give Them a Good Time........................... 51

Tune Down the Music 52

Clean up After Yourself........................... 52

When It Comes to Working with Sensitive Individuals 52

When They Take Something You Said or Did Personally 53

Chapter 7: Living with a Sensitive Child **54**

The Top Qualities of Sensitive Youngsters 55

The Three Most Important Factors to Take into
Consideration When Dealing with a Very Sensitive Child 56

Taking Care of Your Highly Sensitive Child 58

Chapter 8: Being a Highly Sensitive Man 62

Chapter 9: Growing up with Emotional Neglect 64

Understanding the Severity of Ignoring These Emotions........... 65

How Emotional Neglect Influences an Exceptionally
Sensitive Youngster 65

Different ways Emotional Neglect Damages Very
Sensitive Youngsters.. 66

Stages to Recuperating from Emotional Neglect as a Child 69

**Chapter 10: What Does a Highly Sensitive Person Sense
That Others Don't?** 71

Allergies.. 71

Aromas 72

Sounds.. 72

Layered Sounds 72

Lights 73

Tastes 73

Dramatic Weather Changes 74

Air Contamination.. 74

Sensitivity toward Food 74

Immune System Conditions 75

Increased Feeling of Agony 75

Clothing Items.. 75

Chapter 11: Highly Sensitive Individuals and Depression 77

Constant Natural Overstimulation...................................... 77

Awareness of Your Inner Self.. 78

A Rich and Invigorating Life 78

Relational Over-incitement 78

Burdening Reactions.. 79

Chapter 12: Highly Sensitive Individuals and Dipolar Disorder 81

What Is Bipolar Disorder? 82

Why It Is Important to Acknowledge If You Are a
Sensitive Person with Bipolar Issues............................... 82

Adapting to Pressure 83

Chapter 13: Highly Sensitive Individuals and the Loss of a Pet 87

Allow Yourself to Mourn 87

Don't Blame Yourself.. 88

Don't Put up a Wall around Your Emotions 89

Adapt to the New Chapter 89

Take Care of Yourself... 90

Chapter 14: Why It Is Hard for an HSP to Travel 91

The Most Effective Method to Appreciate Travel as
an Exceptionally Sensitive Individual 92

Chapter 15: Best Careers for HSPs.................................... 95

HSPs Need a Vocation That Is Something beyond a Check........... 96

The Best Vocations for Very Sensitive Individuals 98

Chapter 16: Top Nutrients for Highly Sensitive Individuals.......... 102

Magnesium 103

Epsom Salt 103

Valerian... 104

Vitamin C 104

Rescue Remedy 104

Chapter 17: Highly Sensitive Individuals and Exercise **106**

Preparing Your Exercise Routine.................................. 107

Cardio Exercise.. 108

Yoga.. 109

Chapter 18: Having a Look at the Confessions of HSP **111**

I Truly Love Being on My Own 111

I Don't Find Everything That Goes on in Discussions Significant 111

I Lie to Escape Social Circumstances............................. 112

I Get So Overpowered with Clamor and Individuals That I Cry .. 112

There is So Much Going on in My Mind I Feel Crazy 113

I Just Like a Handful of Individuals............................. 113

I Have a Feeling That I'm Faking It When I Meet
New Individuals 113

I'm Superior to My Early Introduction 113

A Ton of Discussions Move Too Rapidly for
My Contemplative Mind to Keep Up................................. 114

I'm Awful at Indicating How I Feel 114

At Times I Wish I Could Vanish 114

I am an Expert in Being Distant from Everyone Else 114

I Quietly Cheer Each Time My Partner Has Plans 114

I Suck at Staying in Contact..................................... 115

**Chapter 19: Debunking the Myths of
Highly Sensitive Individuals**..................................**116**

Very Sensitive Individuals Are Timid............................. 116

Most Exceptionally Sensitive Individuals Are Ladies 117

Being Sensitive Is a Negative Trait 117

In the Event That an Individual is Very Sensitive,
They Don't Share it 117

Exceedingly Sensitive Individuals Decide Whether
to Be Sensitive or Not 118

It's Better Not to Be Exceptionally Sensitive 118

Exceptionally Sensitive Individuals Battle Having Relationships. 118

The Manner in Which an Exceedingly Sensitive Youngster
Is Raised Doesn't Make a Difference 118

Exceptionally Sensitive Individuals Are
Fundamentally the Same 119

Being Exceptionally Sensitive Is Equivalent to Being
Candidly Powerless 119

**Chapter 20: When Is the Right Time to Seek Help
If You Are an HSP?** **120**

Beginning Your Inquiry 120

Finding an Authorized Advisor 121

Where to Look 121

Permit Yourself an opportunity to Choose 122

Chapter 21: Inspirational Quotes for Sensitive Souls **124**

Conclusion **132**

Resources **140**

Chapter 1

What Is a Highly Sensitive Person?

A highly sensitive person can be defined as someone who has a deeper physical, emotional, or mental reaction to certain situations in life. Since sensitivity stems directly from an individual's brain and thoughts, it's an extremely difficult way of living as sensitivity is often misunderstood.

Sensitive behavior can stem from a number of different direct and indirect factors which include the people around individuals, their direct surrounding, as well as an individual's own thoughts and emotions.

While all people feel sensitive at one time or another, each person handles the notion of being sensitive in different ways. Many people experience sensitivity as a fraction of emotion; however, individuals classified as highly sensitive will experience a much greater and deeper response to a certain situation. In some cases, these situations can be overwhelming and cause a sensitive person to feel isolated from what is considered normal behavior.

To rid themselves from these sensitive feelings, individuals often retreat to rather wanting to be alone or isolating themselves in fear of being exposed to more situations where sensitivity can be evoked. For some, isolation can be a great resolution as it gives individuals time to get a hold on their reactions and recuperate their thoughts.

Sensitive people tend to have a deeper understanding and thought process for situations others might find platonic. Being a sensitive person is not something that occurs overnight and often takes a while to get used to. However, sensitive people, although finding themselves different, find ways to cope with being highly sensitive.

Things You Need to Know About Highly Sensitive People

Here are three straightforward, imperative certainties everybody should think about very sensitive individuals:

Being exceedingly sensitive is a typical attribute. Roughly 15 to 20 percent of the world has the quality that makes them exceedingly delicate or sensitive.

High affectability is a genuine trademark. In brain research, any individual who tests as having a high level of sensory preparing sensitivity (SPS), an identity characteristic, is viewed as exceedingly sensitive. SPS is the quality of profoundly preparing encounters and scenarios, and an individual with high SPS has contrasts of the neural dimension.

Being exceptionally sensitive accompanies two focal points and downsides. Very sensitive individuals will, in general, be compassionate, masterfully innovative, instinctive, and exceptionally mindful of the necessities of others—to such an extent that many flourish in professions as advisors, guides, specialists, artists, and journalists. Sensitive individuals likewise manage overpowering, weariness, and burnouts, particularly from "engrossing" or detecting all the emotions of the general population around them. Boisterous, swarmed, or bustling spaces can overpower sensitive individuals.

As a result of their need to invest their energy alone, exceedingly sensitive individuals are frequently mistaken for self-observers. However, anybody can be exceptionally sensitive, regardless of whether they are withdrawn or outgoing.

Science-Based Qualities That Characterize an Exceedingly Sensitive Individual

Thinking about whether you're an HSP? Have a look at these indications of a profoundly sensitive individual.

In the event that you've regularly been informed that you feel things "too" profoundly, are "too" touchy, or that you "feel things excessively," you're likely an exceedingly sensitive individual. (In all actuality, you aren't "too" a lot of anything. You just have an exceptionally extraordinary and incredible identity quality that accompanies the two upsides and downsides.) However, it comprehends the characteristics of a profoundly sensitive individual.

Fortunately, those characteristics have been studied in both people and animals for over twenty years. It gives the idea that a large number of the encounters shared by HSPs come down to only a couple of central attributes. These attributes were initially archived by Dr. Elaine Aron and have been confirmed by different scientists.

Today, Dr. Aron's research centers around four primary characteristics that characterize an exceedingly sensitive individual, spoken to by the abbreviation DOES:

The Profundity of Processing

HSPs will, in general, procedure data more profoundly than others. For instance, when somebody tells an HSP their location, the HSP may rationally rehash it again and again, or contrast the road name with other comparable sounding words and names. They may see an allegorical association between the road name and different thoughts.

This has a viable use—it implies they are probably not going to overlook the location—and it's additionally part of what makes HSPs so masterfully inventive. Be that as it may, it likewise implies that their sensory system is preparing each snippet of data, again and again, frequently amplifying it. This is the primary attribute of exceedingly sensitive individuals, and it's what gives HSPs a feeling of "burnouts" or overburdens.

Below is a layout of the most common feelings HSPs have to deal with on a regular basis:

Overstimulation

Preparing each and every detail, constantly, is debilitating. Since an HSP will take in and consider subtleties that a great many people never see, they are accepted performing more subjective work than the normal individual throughout the day. Therefore, it is normal that an HSP will feel depleted in circumstances where others feel fine.

Examples of this include having the capacity to just arrange a couple of things in a day of movement, an agenda that does not require loads of work, needing a moment of calm without discussion. Individuals who are not HSP, on the other hand, may need to continue talking or prefer a bustling eatery or high-vitality club. HSPs can deal with high-boost situations, just for shorter periods of time.

Sympathy

Passionate reactivity implies that HSPs have a more grounded response to both positive and negative encounters. With that said, research has demonstrated that this impact is especially articulated in connection to positive encounters—or even photos of a positive occasion. Positive settings help rocket HSPs into a passionate state, where better imagination and thinking takes place. This might be a piece of the reason most HSPs try to make a private asylum (which they regularly need nobody else to enter) where they can control their environment and make the air around them their own.

Sympathy implies that HSPs are increasingly mindful of the feelings of others. They consider what other needs and they are worried about helping other people. The mind of a profoundly sensitive individual responds to pictures of other individuals' faces and their "reflect neurons." This is the piece of the cerebrum that encourages us to comprehend and sympathize with the feelings of others.

For an HSP, the experience of sympathy isn't simply "to understand" somebody's feelings. Numerous HSPs feel the need to assimilate feelings when somebody isn't actively communicating them.

Affectability to Nuances

HSPs are naturals with regards to getting unobtrusive signs or boosts that others miss. This doesn't mean they have super-hearing or vision; it's basically what happens when the sensory system is wired to process each detect impression profoundly. The outcome is that HSPs will hear little sounds, modest diversions, scents, or tastes that others don't appear to try and know about. (This can sustain into being overstimulated since most working environments are intended for individuals who aren't diverted or disturbed by such "small" subtleties!)

You may relate to a portion of these qualities more than others. Be that as it may, if you wound up gesturing alongside the majority of sensitive individuals, there's a huge chance you're part of the population classified as HSP.

But HSPs, remember just one thing—you are a normal person, you are in good health, and your identity accompanies some genuine focal points."

The World Needs More Exceptionally Sensitive Individuals

HSPs can flourish; there is no doubt about that. In case you're a very sensitive individual, you're very comfortable with encounters of overpower, stress, and overburden. For numerous HSPs, these overpowering feelings define their entire being and can become a huge burden to carry. Some may stress that something is "broken" inside them, while others basically feel barred by a non-sensitive society. However, your affectability isn't a shortcoming. It's a quality.

Being very sensitive is an impeccably ordinary "thing" to be. Also, if you are exceptionally sensitive, the world needs more individuals precisely like you.

Living in the 21'st century with the world developing and moving at a very fast pace, being a sensitive person can be rather challenging. However, living in this modern day and age while being a highly sensitive person can also be seen as having a huge advantage. With your sensitivity, you can add that something "extra" to any business, any situation and any environment you might find yourself in. For those fresh into adulthood, being highly sensitive means have that edge that puts you a step above the rest.

A great example would be by looking at it from a corporate perspective. A thriving designing company is looking for someone to assist with adding details, new ideas and a fresh approach to the board. A non-sensitive person might apply for the job and have a great imagination to bring ideas to life. However, a sensitive person (although limited in a bustling corporate world) might also apply for the job. Not only does this person have new ideas, this person can also connect with his or her surroundings on a personal level. These sensitive individuals might make a comment about how, instead of a room design facing one way, it should face the other way. Thus, by tapping into their sensitivity to their surroundings, they add an extra layer of creativity to the mix a non-sensitive person might not be able to add.

We Need Very Sensitive Individuals on the Following Grounds

- HSPs see shades of feeling that nobody else sees—and uses them to improve the world. Many people probably won't figure they can identify with high affectability; however, risks are great that their main tunes, works of art and stories were made by the very sensitive. HSPs are supplied with the ability to venture into the universe of emotions and dreams—and distill them as educational glimpses for other people.

- HSPs offer agreeable and caring initiatives. Don't imagine it any other way; while numerous HSPs detest the vicious idea of the business world, others are effectively attempting to transform it. Sensitive pioneers will, in general, listen to their group, express explanations behind their choices and focus on the qualities and inclinations of those they work with. They are enthusiastic about empowering words and building agreement, and they enable workers to vent when required without revile. Profoundly sensitive pioneers might be in the minority, yet they may be the best chiefs (and supervisors) you'll ever have.

- They help everyone around them process their feelings (and get their requirements met). Is it conceivable that profoundly sensitive individuals assume a crucial transformative job— filling in as the "emotional processor" for whatever is left of the gathering? Any individual who companions with an HSP will probably say yes. HSPs fill in as sounding sheets; they develop their companions with consolation, they respond genuinely and sympathetically to your battles and they enable you to see associations you wouldn't have seen with anyone else. HSPs, you are ordinary, you are appreciated, and your identity accompanies some genuine focal points. It isn't easy being exceptionally sensitive and you may need to learn methodologies to adapt to overpowering feelings. Yet there is no doubt about it: Your affectability is your most noteworthy quality.

Indications of Being a Very Sensitive Individual

It is safe to say that you are an exceedingly sensitive individual? Do you know somebody in your own life who might be exceedingly sensitive? High affectability can be characterized as intense physical, mental, and passionate reactions to outside (social, natural) or inward (intra-individual) upgrades. An exceedingly sensitive individual might be a thoughtful person, an outgoing person, or someplace in the middle.

There are numerous constructive parts of being a sensitive individual (for example, a more noteworthy capacity to tune in and avow, more prominent sympathy and instinct or better comprehension of others' needs). In this chapter, we will concentrate on parts of high affectability which antagonistically influence one's well-being, joy, and achievement, and regularly muddle connections. The following are twenty-four indications of a very sensitive individual. While some individuals may adhere to more of these indications than others, it is important to note that sensitivity can be classified at various levels.

While numerous individuals may encounter a portion of these signs every now and then, a very sensitive individual will probably experience these feelings with a high level of emotion. A few people might be exceptionally sensitive to only a couple of improvements, while others might be unequivocally influenced by a number of indications.

Classification One: Affectability about Oneself

- Regularly experiences issues relinquishing negative considerations and feelings

- Every now and again feels physical side effects (for example stress or cerebral pain) when something disagreeable occurs during the day

- Regularly have terrible days that influence eating or potentially dozing propensities in an unfortunate way, for example, eating or dozing excessively

- Regularly encounters strain or tension

- Tends to "beat oneself up" while missing the mark concerning own desires

- Fears dismissal, even in moderately minor circumstances

- Contrasts self as well as other people regularly (in physical, social, social, work, money related, or different situations) and encounters despondent sentiments from antagonistic social examination

- Regularly feels outraged or hatred about circumstances throughout everyday life or in the public eye which appear to be uncalled for, disturbing, or basically irritating

Classification Two: Affectability about Others

- Regularly considers/stresses over what others are considering

- Will, in general, think about things literally

- Thinks that it's troublesome, when activated by moderately little obnoxiousness with individuals, to simply "let it go"

- Feels hurt effectively

- Frequently conceals negative sentiments, trusting they are excessively solid, fierce, humiliating or helpless against offer; keeps a great deal of negative feelings inside

- On the other hand, frequently examines negative feelings with others on the grounds that there's a great deal of "dramatization" in one's life

- Experiences serious difficulties tolerating basic input, notwithstanding when it's given sensibly and usefully

- Regularly feels like individuals are judgmental, notwithstanding when there's no solid proof

- Frequently blows up to genuine or saw insults and incitements

- Regularly feels clumsy in gathering circumstances and feels helpless to act naturally

- Feels reluctant in impractically personal circumstances; too many stresses over accomplice's endorsement; is nonsensically terrified of being judged or dismissed by an accomplice

Classification Three: Affectability about One's Condition

- Feels awkward in huge open groups, in a room brimming with individuals talking, or when an excessive number of things are happening all the while

- Feels awkward when presented to brilliant lights, uproarious sounds, or certain solid aromas

- Startles effectively at sudden clamors, quick traffic or other upsetting astonishments

- Regularly feels upset when watching or perusing negative news in the media. Aversions "stun" stimulation (for example strongly unnerving or vicious shows)

- Regularly feels despondent when following individuals' posts via web-based networking media

For some exceedingly sensitive individuals, the way to overseeing oversensitivity is to use enthusiastic invulnerability and tangible resistance procedures to ease overstimulation. For the individuals who live or work with very sensitive people, powerful relational abilities are an unquestionable requirement to encourage constructive and helpful connections.

Chapter 2

Self-Tests to Find out If You Are a Highly Sensitive Person

Sensation-Seeking Test

Answer each inquiry as per the manner in which you feel. Answer truthfully and in any event to some degree valid for you. Answer false in the event that it isn't extremely valid or true under any condition valid for you.

- If I felt protected, I might want to take a medication that would make me have bizarre new encounters.

- I can turn out to be horrendously exhausted in a few discussions.

- I would prefer to go to another spot I dislike than return again to a spot I realize I like.

- I might want to attempt a game that makes a physical rush, such as skiing, shake climbing, or surfing.

- I get irritated in the event that I remain home for long.

- I don't care getting held up with nothing to do.

- I watch a motion picture more than once.

- I appreciate the new.

- In the event that I see something uncommon, I will make a special effort to look at it.

- I get exhausted investing energy with similar individuals.

- My companions state it is difficult to foresee what I will do.

- I like to investigate other territories.

- I abstain from having a day-by-day schedule.

- I am attracted to workmanship that gives me extreme satisfaction.

- I like substances that make me feel "high."

- I lean toward companions who are unusual.

- I anticipate being in a spot that is new and abnormal to me.

- When I spend money on travel, I would opt for a foreign nation to enjoy my trip.

- I might want to be a pilgrim.

- I appreciate it when somebody makes a surprising sexual joke or remark that gets everybody chuckling a little anxiously.

The Sensation-Seeker Test Results for Ladies

If addressed consistent with at least eleven of the inquiries, you're likely a sensation seeker. In the event that you addressed consistent with seven or less of the inquiries, you are most likely not a sensation seeker. If you addressed consistent with eight, nine, or ten of the inquiries, you are most likely someplace in the middle of being sensation seeking.

The Sensation-Seeker Test Results for Men

In the event that you addressed consistent with at least thirteen of the inquiries, you're most likely a sensation seeker. If you addressed consistent with nine or less of the inquiries, you are presumably not a sensation seeker. If you addressed consistent with ten, eleven, or twelve of the inquiries, you are most likely someplace in the middle of being a sensation seeker.

Highly Sensitive Child Test

It would be ideal if you answer each inquiry as well as can be expected. Check all answers if it is valid, and leave questions blank if it is not valid for your child or was for a generous time previously.

My youngster exhibits the following characteristics or habits:

- Gets startled easily

- Whines about a scratchy dress, creases in socks, or marks against his/her skin

- Doesn't, as a rule, appreciate huge amazement

- Prefers a delicate remedy over solid discipline

- Appears to peruse my brain

- Uses huge words for his/her age

- Takes note of the scarcest bizarre smell

- Has a cunning comical inclination

- Appears to be inquisitive

- Does not settle down to sleep easily after a long day

- Doesn't do well with huge changes

- Needs to change garments if wet or sandy

- Solicits parts from inquiries

- Is a stickler

- Takes note of the trouble of others

- Leans toward a calm play

- Asks profound, intriguing questions

- Is sensitive to torment

- Is pestered by boisterous spots

- Takes note of nuances (something that has been moved or an adjustment in an individual's appearance)

- Considers a space protected and safe before walking or moving along it

- Performs best when outsiders are absent

- Feels things profoundly

Test Results

If you addressed consistent with at least thirteen of the inquiries, your youngster is most likely exceptionally sensitive. In any case, no mental test is accurate to the point that you should base how you treat your youngster on it. In the event that just a single or two inquiries are valid for your child, yet they are very valid, you may likewise be advocated in calling your youngster profoundly sensitive.

Am I a Highly Sensitive Person Test

Answer each inquiry as per the manner in which you feel. Check each question in the event that it is at any rate to some degree valid for you and leave unchecked in the event that it isn't valid or not in any manner valid for you.

- I am overpowered by solid, tangible info.

- I am, by all accounts, mindful of nuances in my condition.

- Other individuals' states of mind influence me.

- I will, in general, be sensitive to torment.

- I wind up expecting to pull back amid occupied days, into bed or into an obscured room or wherever I can have some security and help from incitement.

- I am especially sensitive to the impacts of caffeine.

- I am overpowered by things like splendid lights, solid scents, coarse textures or alarms close by.

- I have a rich, complex internal life.

- I feel awkward near noisy commotions.

- I am profoundly moved by expressions of human experience or music.

- My sensory system feels so fatigued that I simply need to go off without anyone else's input.

- I am faithful.

- I startle easily.

- I get shaken when I have a great deal to do in a short measure of time.

- At the point when individuals are awkward in a physical domain, I will, in general, realize what should be done to make it progressively agreeable (like changing the lighting or the seating).

- I am irritated when individuals attempt to inspire me to do an excessive number of things all at once.

- I make a decent attempt to abstain from committing errors or overlooking things.

- I make a point to stay away from fierce motion pictures and network programs.

- I turn out to be negatively stimulated when a ton is going on around me.

- Being extremely eager makes a solid response in me, disturbing my fixation or inclination.

- Changes throughout my life shake me up.

- I see and appreciate fragile or fine aromas, tastes, sounds, and masterpieces.

- I think that it's horrendous to have a ton going on without a moment's delay.

- I make it a high need to master my life to abstain from disquieting or overpowering circumstances.

- I am pestered by extraordinary improvements, boisterous clamors or disorderly scenes.

- When I should contend or be watched while playing out an assignment, I turn out to be so apprehensive or flimsy that I do much more awful than I would something else.

- When I was a kid, my folks or educators appeared to consider me to be sensitive or bashful.

Test Results

If you addressed more than fourteen of the inquiries as valid for yourself, you are most likely exceedingly sensitive. Yet no mental test is accurate to the point that an individual should put together his or her existence with respect to it. In the event that fewer inquiries are valid for you, yet very obvious, that may likewise legitimize calling you profoundly sensitive. However, despite the fact that there a number of men and ladies who are exceptionally sensitive, when stepping through the examination, very sensitive men answer marginally fewer things as valid than do profoundly sensitive ladies.

Chapter 3

Sensitivity, Your Body, and Your Brain

By now, it might be clear that you understand what the main difference between an HSP and other people are. Thus, it is safe to say that the mind of a highly sensitive person does not function in the same way as others may.

For the most part, this is hereditary. There are various qualities that clarify whether somebody is very sensitive, and each of these has to do with your body, mind, and emotions when entering a specified situation.

A very sensitive cerebrum is directly affected by nearby surroundings. The primary quality that makes you exceptionally sensitive makes you progressively responsive to ecological impacts, particularly in youth. For that reason, it is important to nurture a young child more if he/she is highly sensitive as it serves a positive impact—even more so as it would have with a non-sensitive child.

So what precisely makes the cerebrum and sensory system of an HSP unique? Let's have a look at the mind of a highly sensitive person to investigate.

What Makes an HSP's Brain Different?

An HSP's Brain Takes to Dopamine in a Different Way

Dopamine is the mind's reward, or adrenaline. It's what makes you "need" to do certain things, and after that vibe, a feeling of triumph kicks in when you do them. However, a significant number of the qualities engaged with high affectability influence how your body utilizes dopamine—in manners we don't completely understand yet. HSPs are less determined by outside sources, which is a piece of what enables them to keep calm and be attentive and perceptive while they process data. That would, likewise, help keep HSPs from being attracted to unfavorable circumstances that end up overpowering them.

In case you're an HSP, and you simply don't like the notion of attending a boisterous gathering, you have your brain's dopamine to thank—it's helping you stay away from overstimulation and burnouts.

The Mirror Neurons in Your Brain Are More Active

Mirror neurons enable you to comprehend what someone else is doing or what they're encountering in light of their activities. They do that by contrasting the other individual's conduct and times they have acted that way—viably "reflecting" the other individual to make sense of what's happening to them.

That is a vital activity for plenty of reasons and enables us to feel sympathy and empathy for other people. When we perceive the torment (or bliss) somebody is experiencing and identify with it, our mirror neurons are the heroes in the scene. More mirror neuron action implies an increasingly compassionate individual—like an HSP.

HSPs don't really have more mirror neurons than others. The only difference is that their mirror neuron frameworks are increasingly active. In 2014, useful cerebrum imaging research found that HSPs had reliably larger amounts of action in key parts of the mind identified with social and passionate handling. A more elevated amount of movement kicked in even in tests including outsiders, exhibiting HSPs' capacity to stretch out empathy to individuals they don't actually know.

As a very sensitive individual, these mirror neurons are both your superpower and, on occasion, your curse—for example the notion of an HSP not being able to watch a movie that seems brutal but that is enjoyed by non-sensitive viewers. But at the same time, it's what makes you warm, mindful, and unbelievably wise about what other individuals are experiencing.

Your Emotions Create a Window Others Do Not Get to Experience

One critical part of your mind, the ventromedial prefrontal cortex (vmPFC) is snared into a framework that includes your feelings, your qualities, and the processing of tangible information. When stating that sensitive individuals "process things more profoundly than others," it is the direct work of the vmPFC.

While every single function of the vmPFC is not yet known, it's unquestionably connected with control—and it enhances the things we get involved in with a passionate "clarity." Everybody encounters life distinctively amid thrilling moments, not only HSPs. High affectability is connected to a quality that builds this striking ability, basically "turning up the dial." That quality enables emotions to have a bigger impact on the vmPFC as it is met with different encounters.

You Are More Aware of Individuals around You

For many less sensitive individuals, it's anything but difficult to block out other individuals. However, for an HSP, nearly everything about the cerebrum is wired around seeing and translating others.

This is obvious from the numerous parts of the cerebrum that get additional information for HSPs in a social setting. For instance, the cerebrum imaging study referenced above didn't simply indicate more prominent action in territories related to compassion. It additionally demonstrated expanded action in the cingulate territory and the insula—two zones that, together, structure the "seat of cognizance" and everyday mindfulness. For HSPs, these regions help form emotional images of other individuals, particularly those showing a significant social or passionate outer core.

At the end of the day, exceptionally sensitive individuals turn out to be increasingly alert, nearly "progressively cognizant," in a social setting. In case you're an HSP, other individuals are the most splendid thing on your radar.

Having a Highly Sensitive Mind Is a Gift

There's a great deal that can be said about the blessings of the exceptionally sensitive mind. It forms data in a more profound way, sees more associations and considerations, and identifies with others significantly. In case you're an exceptionally sensitive individual, your cerebrum might be the most dominant social weapon in the known universe.

Perhaps your most critical blessing as an HSP is the one intended to secure you. Your mind is tweaked to see and decipher the conduct of everybody around you. In the event that somebody gets terrible news, you know it. In the event that somebody doesn't treat you right, you see it coming. What's more, if specific circumstances aren't favorable for you, you realize that as well.

That is fundamental, on the grounds that an exceptionally sensitive individual needs a stable environment and steady friends and family so as to flourish—maybe much more so than others.

In case you're an exceedingly sensitive individual, trust your instinct. Your mind is your ally, and it's pulling for you.

The Reason Behind an HSP Absorbing Other People's Emotions

HSPs have a massive limit with respect to sympathy. Because of this characteristic, we will, in general, be attracted to helping others, and we frequently progress toward becoming guardians for our loved ones. Our sympathy frequently outperforms that of the ordinary meaning of the word. Instead of just detecting what another person is feeling, a large number of us really begin feeling it ourselves.

As debilitating as it very well may be to assimilate the feelings of others, it tends to be an advantage in occupations that require a little perusing. When this characteristic begins working at rapid, it turns out to be sincerely debilitating, making us feeling like our tank is on a void.

Let's have a look at why numerous HSPs assimilate the sentiments of others and how they can quit being so depleted by it.

All HSPs will, in general, be very influenced by the feelings of others. A large number of HSPs can stroll into a room and promptly sense pressure, bliss, inconvenience, and pity with no verbal correspondence. As it were, they are ace nonverbal communicators.

However, it's more than that—it resembles they can simply "sense" feeling. Most HSPs have encountered something along the lines of being with a companion, knowing the feeling they are encountering and waiting for them to speak up about how they are feeling. This is one reason HSPs loathe struggle so much: They can detect it coming and experience the sentiments of the other individual just as their own.

These feelings don't remain separate from them. Numerous HSPs would battle to enter even a marginally tense environment and not feel tense themselves. While the vast majority can get on the feelings of others to some degree—on account of mirror neurons—for HSPs, the experience is significantly different.

Accordingly, they may end up feeling bad-tempered or dormant. At the point when this begins, it's regularly because of one of two things: It is possible that they are grabbing on the feeling of the other individual and making it their own, or they have effectively gone up against this weight of feeling and in their mind, is disclosing to their own burnout from conveying another person's weight.

Prioritizing Your Needs

To help you better understand the entire scenario, let's have a look at an example of an experience of an HSP therapist (who is an HSP herself), and for the sake of the scenario, let us call this therapist Jane. As an HSP specialist, she found it important for her to figure out how to complete two things: prioritize and set limits.

Amid the primary months of her temporary job, she always felt depleted, panicky before observing customers, and depleted a short time later. She pondered over her customers almost constantly and planned their sessions late in the evening as opposed to resting. She persuaded herself that she should have been sincerely associated with her customers so as to cultivate change.

In sessions, her very own uneasiness may rise when the feelings in the room heightened. Be that as it may, as her customer load grew, she turned out to be all the more tolerating of her feelings of anxiety and ended up used to living at that dimension of fatigue and tension.

In the meantime, her own capacity to control her own feelings began slipping. It was then when she genuinely understood the need to prioritize. That was the point at which she felt how much the feelings of her customers were affecting her, despite the fact that she thought she was absolutely fine. It wasn't until she ceased and rested for a minute that she understood exactly how profound her weariness was.

This issue continued into different aspects of her life, as does the arrangement. Some sensitive individuals may see this issue in their associations with companions, family, collaborators and even the cashier at the supermarket. HSPs realize when something isn't right with an individual—it resembles their intuition.

On the grounds that we sense somebody needs assistance does not mean we discredit the directly to think about ourselves. You can do this by turning your telephone on silent mode during the evening and giving yourself the authorization to request help when you need it. Requesting help can be particularly troublesome for HSPs, in light of the fact that they would prefer not to load other individuals. Much the same as they help other people, they can request help themselves. All things considered, they can't adequately help if their very own lives are burdened by that of others.

Why HSPs Need Sound Boundaries

Organizing self-care is just the initial phase in helping you defeat weariness. You additionally need to define better boundaries. Let's make use of Jane's situation once more: When she previously began seeing customers, she didn't completely get a handle on the need to isolate her own feelings from those of her customers. Compassion places her in someone else's shoes for sixty minutes, yet after that hour, their feelings need to return to being completely their own.

Learning ways to keep work at work has been fundamental in dealing with her situation. In helping others, it's particularly hard to make these limits, since she works with individuals every day. Saying no is inconceivably hard, particularly when, as an HSP, Jane detected the feelings of her customers.

The equivalent goes in your own connections. At the point when HSPs deal with loved ones, it's difficult to close off that ingestion. You have an obligation to tune in and help, yet you don't have an obligation to be gobbled up by the sentiments of others.

Defining boundaries in expert and individual connections is a test, yet it tends to be fulfilling. There's an alleviation that accompanies putting a limit on your assistance, to giving yourself consent to say no, to just get a decent night's rest as opposed to conversing with a companion for an hour or more during the evening. The issue will be there at the beginning of a new day.

Obviously, there are times when boundaries should be adaptable; however, in those circumstances, the boundary can look like setting aside time for self-care a while later.

Jane, for instance, found that she felt a gigantic feeling of blame when she was not going up against the feelings of someone else. Be that as it may, not surrendering to the impulse to retain her customer's feelings just to make herself feel like she's working to the perfection of aiding is a limit in itself.

Tolerating that she had the ability to define that boundary, to hear her out body and mind when it's requesting a vacation day, has been instrumental in continuing her quest—and is something all HSPs will profit by grasping.

Chapter 4

What Do Highly Sensitive People Need to Be Happy?

Since being a highly sensitive person requires more intense ways of keeping a healthy mental state, it is important to select a number of ways to keep a happy state of mind. But what exactly does an HSP need in order to be happy?

An HSP Needs to Live a Slow-Paced Life

This should not be taken as an HSP not wanting to do as much work as a non-sensitive person. An HSP feels things more deeply, and thus, they do more work than a non-sensitive person would on a day-to-day basis. Since sensitive individuals take in so much data, simple tasks may take longer to complete. For example, a non-sensitive person would go to the supermarket and purchase a chicken casserole without thinking twice. A sensitive person, on the other hand, may ponder for a few minutes while staring at the casserole on the shelf. They might be thinking of a chicken being held in a coop for days while then being taken to get slaughtered. That might make them think twice about having that specific casserole for dinner.

An HSP Needs Time to Rest After a Long Day

Since sensitive individuals process loads of information during the day while having to deal with thousands of smells, sensations, and feelings, they need time to wind down and relax their mind after a busy day. The feeling of being overwhelmed might have snuck up on them a few times during the day, and for that reason, it is important for a sensitive person seeking a happy and healthy state of mind to take a load off when work is done.

An HSP Needs a Safe Haven to Relax

For some people, a drink after work at a local club is the best way to unwind. However, for sensitive individuals, a relaxing corner in their home (or under the covers) is the best place to call their "happy place." From here, they can read a book, listen to music, or snuggle up to a light-hearted movie. Contentment is what comes to mind when looking at HSPs in this environment.

An HSP Needs to Know It's All Right to Cry and Get Emotional

There is not a thing in the world more excruciating than an HSP having to hold back their tears simply because their companion of friend does not like it when they cry. In order for an HSP to rid themselves of excessive feelings that bubble over, they need to know it is all right to get emotional and cry. After wiping their tears, they will feel much better and look at the world with a fresh sense of courage.

An HSP Needs the Time to Absorb Changes

For some individuals, moving into a new home, finding a new companion, or changing jobs might be something exciting and thrilling. For an HSP, it isn't all fun and games. Although it is nearly impossible for them to avoid these types of situations, they need extra time to adjust to their new setting or situation. Since they need to process a load of new information that will keep their minds overwhelmed for a while, they need time to sort through every detail in order to go on with a happy and healthy mindset.

An HSP Needs to Make Close, Important Connections

HSPs ache for profound associations with others. Indeed, they may get exhausted or fretful seeing someone that needs interaction. Nonetheless, this doesn't imply that they're inclined to relationship jumping. On the contrary, they might rather want to strike up a conversation that might interest both in order to establish closeness and a potential connection.

This, likewise, implies HSPs will be specific about the general population they let into their lives. A straightforward surface-level, give-and-take relationship will not cut it for an HSP. They need to jump into your spirit and associate with you significantly.

An HSP Needs a Solid Method of Handling Conflict

HSP or not, battling with a friend or family member is terrible; however, sensitive individuals will, in general, feel additional on edge when conflict emerges. Frequently, an inner fight will also ensue. The HSP may have solid emotions about something; however, they hush about them since they would prefer not to make the other individual frantic. Managing an irate individual can be overstimulating.

Besides, we despise harming other individuals since we know, from individual experience, exactly how deliberating that is. HSPs will have elevated amounts of sympathy, and this is only one of the manners in which our thinking about others appears.

Sadly, this implies sensitive individuals regularly shroud their requirements and simply "agree to get along." They need a sound method for managing differences that don't include shouting or violence.

An HSP Needs a Decent Night's Rest

An absence of rest is sufficient to make anybody crotchety, messy and very ineffective. Be that as it may, an absence of rest for an HSP can make life terrible, to say the very least. Getting enough rest mitigates the HSPs sloped up faculties and enables them to process their feelings. How much rest a sensitive individual gets can truly represent the deciding moment of their entire day.

It's easy for a non-sensitive person to survive on only a few hours of sleep for a couple of days before trying to catch up on those lost hours. Yes, they might become a little cranky but for a sensitive person, it could mean the difference between keeping it together or completely losing it. Without a good night's rest every night, a sensitive person will find it very hard to function and will also feel miserable about the fact that they did not sleep well. Combine that with the hypersensitivity to be a perfectionist when you know you just can't and you've got a full-on sensitive mess on your hands.

An HSP Needs to Maintain a Healthy Diet throughout the Day

Craving can truly upset a sensitive individual's inclination or focus. HSPs are the perfect definitive of angry when they don't eat well and eat regularly. With that said, caffeine and alcohol might make them even more sensitive, so it is never a good idea to cheer an HSP up with it.

An HSP Needs to Have an Outlet for Their Inventive Side

Numerous HSPs have a solid need to create. They channel their piercing perceptions, experiences, and feelings into workmanship, verse, music, and more. Sensitivity can be overpowering, yet it is likewise similar to having additional space on a hard drive. Inventiveness is the weight valve for all things that overwhelm a sensitive soul.

An HSP Needs a Solid Feeling of Direction

A few people appear to float through existence without bearing or reason. For HSPs, this is unfathomable. Or maybe, they contemplate the huge things throughout everyday life. Who are they, for what reason would they say they are here and what were they put on this planet to do? Regardless of whether it's composing a novel, venturing to the far corners of the planet, or driving the route for a reason they have faith in, HSPs long for importance.

An HSP Needs Friends and Family Who Understand and Regard Their Sensitive Nature

Since many people are not sensitive, they don't always understand what it resembles to get very worried by, for example, a startling commotion, a bustling weekend or a rough scene in a motion picture. Not every person will understand, and that is all right. What an HSP needs is somewhere around a couple of individuals—ideally the general population nearest to them—to "get" their sensitivity. Somebody who gets it yet shields them from overstimulation as well as

34

somebody who sees all the great endowments that accompany this uncommon characteristic.

An HSP Needs a Glimpse of Nature Every Now and Then

HSP or not, our condition influences us. For instance, individuals will, in general, feel more joyful in rooms with bent edges and adjusted shapes than in sharp-edged rectangular rooms. Likewise, green spaces support our inclination to alleviate psychological instability. For HSPs, this impact is significant. For them, the manner in which things look truly matters. Jumbled, tumultuous or outright terrible situations may truly disrupt them. Excellence is a spirit medicine that revives and mitigates.

A sensitive person gets a huge wave of relaxation and inner-strength from listening to a slight breeze through the leaves of a tree, the waves crashing on the shoreline or frogs croaking in the distance. This kind of tranquility is what makes sensitive minds feel at peace and ready to take on the world once more.

Chapter 5

How to Live with Being a Highly Sensitive Person

Highly sensitive individuals are often seen as powerless or broken. Yet to feel powerless isn't a side effect of shortcoming; it is just a normal reaction of a truly compassionate individual. It isn't the sensitive individual who is broken; it is society's understanding that is debilitated. There is zero disgrace in communicating your true emotions. The individuals who are, on occasion, portrayed as being "excessively passionate" or "muddled" are the very texture of what keeps the fantasy alive for a caring and thoughtful world. Never be embarrassed to let your emotions and tears shed a welcoming light in this world.

With that said, being a highly sensitive person can become confusing at times and cause individuals to ponder on a few questions such as: Why do I get overpowered by ordinary undertakings that others take in their stride? Why do I consider insults that should be overlooked? Why are nuances amplified for me but lost on others?

It resembles you were brought into the world missing a defensive layer of skin that others appear to have.

You attempt to conceal it. Numb it. Block it out. However, the remarks still penetrate your defensive layer: "You're overthinking things. You're excessively sensitive. Toughen up!"

You're left pondering what on earth might be the matter with you. You yearn for that faces the same situations as you and think about things the same way you do. Won't it be wonderful to hear the words, "You feel the same way? So do I!"

Numerous sensitive individuals feel disengaged from others. They feel misconstrued and abnormal and then often don't have the foggiest idea why. They simply don't understand that they have a basic characteristic that clarifies their peculiarities.

Upon doing a little research of your own, you might find that many famous figures over the ages were indeed highly sensitive individuals. Albert Einstein, Martin Luther King, and Steve Jobs all had the powerful gift of being sensitive people. Any HSP would consider this to be incredible news since it implies that sensitive souls aren't innately hindered.

However, when we don't understand how to deal with our affectability, we end up pushing too hard to even consider keeping up with other individuals. We endeavor to do what others appear to deal with effortlessly and attempt to show improvement over them. What's more, this prompts issues.

For a period, we complete a top-notch occupation of utilizing our regular blessings: we're inventive understudies and principled representatives. But when we hammer on past our cut-off points, we can cause ourselves significant physical injury. It appears in the form of muscle or joint pressures we can't dispose of and being unendingly exhausted or nervous without any justifiable cause.

In the event that you reverberate with any of this, here are ten ways you, as a sensitive individual, can make use of to quit battling and begin flourishing:

Stop Hunting Down Somebody or Something to Fix You

Sensitivity or being sensitive has to do with your temperament and should not be seen as a medicinal issue. Thus, nothing is naturally amiss with you. Tragically, however, many professionals don't comprehend this in light of the fact that tactile handling sensitivity, researching this emotional state is still in its infancy.

Of course, very sensitive individuals are bound to have hypersensitivities or sensitivities to nourishment, synthetic substances as well as prescriptions. Furthermore, they're progressively inclined to overstimulation, along these lines finding it easier to feel pressure— which can prompt other medical problems. However, sensitivity in itself isn't something that needs settling but rather ways of coping with sensitive situations.

Individuals who handle their sensitive nature with ease understand that they're not "broken." If your psyche is depleted from hectically investigating one more answer to remove your "blemishes," realize that the responses to living in amicability with your sensitive nature live inside you.

Let Yourself Know That You Are Not Fake

Impostor disorder isn't selective to exceedingly sensitive individuals. Numerous high accomplishing individuals succumb to this annoying apprehension. Yet the stewing distress about being discovered is consistent for a sensitive individual.

Is there any good reason it wouldn't be, considering you've spent a lifetime of feeling different from others and endeavoring to fit in? Perhaps you accuse the tears in your eyes amid that television ad, or you agree to accept the organization fun run despite the fact that you detest running and you realize you'll feel embarrassed about what extent your body will take to recoup. Regardless of whether you grew up showing your sensitivity with satisfaction, it's improbable you got away from the social weight inspiring you to camouflage your genuine self to fit the standards of others.

Flourishing sensitive individuals regard that their sensory systems are wired uniquely in contrast to 80–85 percent of individuals. Honing your accomplishments and qualities enables you to show the real you.

Search for Like-Minded People and Realize That You are Not the Only One

You feel overpowered by society, and you feel alone. However, in all actuality, you're most certainly not. Many have encountered disarray in segregation before finding that crowds of individuals have some sense of what it resembles to be you. They've felt the flood of intensity that originates from being bolstered by like-minded people. Also, they need to show proactive kindness.

The key is to spend time with sensitive individuals who are thriving, or if nothing else, open to those potential outcomes. They comprehend how to deal with their sensitivity, yet they know how to employ its superpowers. They comprehend what it resembles for you to feel under attack, and they can offer firsthand involvement and insight to enable you to make your sensitivities work to support you.

Thriving sensitives acknowledge and relish the qualities of sensitivity in themselves as well as other people. In case you're feeling unsupported or misconstrued, discover a sensitively proficient mentor, tutor, or network who gets you and support that association.

Search for the Concealed Energy in Each Circumstance and Relish in It

The cerebrum is an incredible channel that molds encounters and views of the real world. In the event that you think the world is an unsafe place, your cerebrum is wired to chase after proof of a threat. If you trust it's a safe spot, you can train yourself to search for spots similar to this. What you center around, you get a greater amount of.

As an exceedingly sensitive individual, the more negative the earth, the more you endure. However, the inverse is also valid—the more positive, the more you flourish; even when it is in contrast with others.

The act of thinking is a way to stimulate your sensory system. As a sensitive person, you need to learn to recognize the negative but not overlook it and then release it. Inundate yourself in positive musings and circumstances that make you feel better, or possibly give you a mitigating liberating sensation.

Thriving sensitives choose to see the world overflowing with chances to feel appreciative for and to relish in that positive vibe. In case you're feeling helpless amid certain conditions, understand that your contemplations and the passionate charges they trigger are at your command.

Find New Ways to Deal with Old Tricks

Your endowments of sensitivity incorporate profound reflection and intuition to see all points and outcomes. By being profound, you're effectively overpowered and depleted by incitement. Also, when you don't comprehend why you feel and act in the manners in which you do, it's anything but difficult to outline these as defects.

In truth, these "shortcomings" are just your neglected need for support. In reframing your past and supporting your present, you set yourself up for achievement in your future.

Thriving sensitives reconsider old observations in light of their more profound understandings of sensitivity. In case you're overloaded by the hypersensitive and ignored parts of yourself, look to find the opposite side of the situation where you'll discover a portion of your most noteworthy qualities: instinct, vision, and honesty.

Treat Yourself with Sympathy

As a very sensitive individual, you are profoundly caring—to such an extent that putting others' needs before your very own is second nature. What's more, you're regularly your own greatest commentator. You propel yourself hard, and after that, you beat yourself up when you come up short. You scrutinize yourself in manners you'd never dream of doing to others.

Controlling your bothering feelings is fundamental to self-empathy. However, as opposed to prevalent thinking, you shouldn't do so by disregarding it. Profound thinking is of your endowments, so why not grasp that control? Take control by listening to your musings without judgment and afterward rotating to contemplations that trigger kinder

41

and more cherishing feelings in your body. From that "feel better" place, you're ready to live positively.

Thriving HSP demonstrates to themselves the equivalent cherishing sympathy that they're normally great at giving others. It might feel childish or vain at first; however, it's most certainly not. In the event that your basic internal voice is cheapening your identity, answer back with self-generosity as this is the antitoxin.

Create Boundaries That Aren't Ridden with Emotion

We live in a culture that qualities "take a painkiller and push on" undeniably more than it esteems sensitivity. We grow up hearing, "No agony, no increase," "Survival of the fittest," "Life isn't fair, so get used to it." We appreciate the individuals who show coarseness to beat their awful predicaments.

As an exceptionally sensitive individual, your reflex response might be to solidify up or battle to toughen up. You create walls to shield yourself from hurt. Emotional walls, for example, can be smothering sentiments or making sensational strife to occupy from the genuine reasons for agony. Physical walls, for example, can be heaped on layers of work to take cover behind. Mental walls, for example, can be blocking out everything around you with liquor or medications.

You may give every one of your limits a chance to fall without a moment's delay, along these lines unwittingly engrossing others' energies and feeling eaten up by their feelings. You endeavor to get away from the emotions by becoming involved with overthinking everything: perpetually arranging and investigating while putting some distance between your instincts. So you beat yourself up about how you realize you ought to have better limits. It's an endless loop.

Thriving sensitives exemplify delicate yet firm limits. If you battle to put your own needs first, which doesn't fall into place easily for a very sensitive individual, settle on a cognizant decision to rehearse the aptitude of saying "no" with adoration and elegance or cutting out alone time to energize and choose to like that.

Listen to What Your Body Tells You in Order to Avoid Emotional Strain

Numerous very sensitive individuals figure out how to disregard the messages their bodies are sending them. They change it to evade overpower, or they check out others' needs rather than their very own to meet what's anticipated of them. Does this sound like you?

Doing this abandons you swinging like a pendulum. Not listening to your body swings you forward and backward between being over-animated and mind-numbingly exhausted, counting calories and after that gorging or practicing hard and afterward requiring a few days to recoup.

Thriving sensitive individuals check out the physical sensations in their bodies; they acknowledge that it's not constantly agreeable, yet they trust their bodies to direct them. If you have a propensity for escaping emotions or passing the purpose of overpower, figure out how to perceive your body's unpretentious indications of overstimulation. You'll invest less energy being tossed out of parity and additional time influencing your sensory system's scope of ideal excitement.

Make Use of Healthy Habits

In the long run, everything catches with you. Overwhelming hours at work, trailed by hard perspiration at the gym and keeping things afloat in your home—all powered by horrible weight control plans and insignificant rest or downtime. It's a simple snare to fall into on the grounds that you're essentially living the manner in which you see the vast majority get by on.

In addition, some unhealthy habits can take its toll on a sensitive sensory system—like nourishments that are vigorously handled and siphoned with sugar and fake substances, or exercise that is not accompanied with sufficient recuperation time.

If you permit excessive incitements without rest in between, you risk getting sick. However, if you overprotect yourself, your virtuoso goes unexpressed, and that, likewise, can prompt your well-being to be put into jeopardy.

Thriving sensitive individuals practice propensities that really support them. In the event that you battle with vitality or prosperity issues, organize propensities that support these parts of your life (for example, more rest and alone time), and a point of confinement if something over-invigorates you (for example, an excessive number of high weights exercises—regardless of whether they are allegedly sound).

Don't Try to Suppress Your Sensitivity

After a lifetime of being shelled by stimuli, it turns out to be second nature to drive sensitivity out of the conscious mind. You, for example, block out certain sensations, for instance, so you can imagine you don't care at all. You condition down extreme emotions (great and awful), so you aren't on a crazy ride. You smother feelings to get a break from everything and everyone around you.

This self-defensive instrument may trick your conscious personality, yet it doesn't trick your sensitive body. This affects your well-being, your connections, your vocation—in short, each part of your life—and it manufactures strain until something's got to give.

Thriving sensitives let go of the grip for control. When you free the vitality used to hold on tight, you free the blessings of sensitivity that have been lost to you: sympathy, imagination, and elevated satisfaction, to give some examples. What's more, you enable your actual potential to bloom.

Remember that the way to flourishing as a very sensitive individual, more than all else, is to perceive that it's all right to be sensitive—with its difficulties and qualities.

Utilize your profound brain to perceive shrouded understandings, and purposely refocus on energy and conceivable outcomes.

Utilize your profound body to tune in your feelings and sensations, and remain in your ideal scope of excitement as frequently as could reasonably be expected.

Utilize your increased attention to move to whatever beat you. It would be ideal for you regardless of whether it appears to be odd to many individuals.

Chapter 6

How to Live with a Highly Sensitive Person

If you think that it's only highly sensitive people who need to take a deeper look at life, you need to realize that in order for them to thrive, you need to be able to do your part as well. Living with an HSP is not easy, yet it gives you the ability to get a glimpse of what goes on in their extraordinary minds. With that said, there is no need to handle them as if they might break at any point. By all means, there is no reason for you to change your outlook on life at all when living with a sensitive soul. All you need to do is make a few adjustments to enable you both to thrive together.

Below are a number of ways you can accommodate living with a sensitive person.

Talk in a Soft Tone When You Are Near Them

Sensitive people tend to startle easily, and loud noises can be emotionally and, at times, even physically painful to them. Sensitive people have the capability to withstand a certain amount of noise, but when it becomes too crowded for them with a huge bustle of sounds, they simply can't keep up with it all. With that said, it is better to use your indoor voice when living with a sensitive person.

Sensitive People Don't Complain as Much as You Might Think

For sensitive individuals, the world is very overwhelming, and there isn't a lot they can do to stop it. Thus, they will get irritated easily and will not hesitate to speak out about their irritation with whatever is going on around them. Keep in mind that they are not trying to constantly complain about everything; they simply want you to understand things from their perspective.

Sensitive Individuals Are Huge Art Lovers

While some people might find sensitive individual's hair color or clothing taste a little odd, it is just a way for them to step into their own comfort zone without being judged by others. Some sensitive individuals might love nude paintings and can lose themselves in the image for a long period of time before snapping back to reality. For them, it a way of healing and not a way of making others think they are strange.

Sensitive Individuals Do Not Like the Feeling of Being Drunk

Should you, along with a sensitive individual, go out to a party, do not pressure them into taking more drinks than they want to have. For non-sensitive individuals, it might be fun to feel tipsy or drunk, but for a sensitive individual, a drunken state isn't very pleasurable. For them, it feels like a headache and the sooner they can ride themselves of it, the better. Thus, if you and your sensitive companion go out and you want to party a little longer, make sure your companion has a way to get home without having to endure long hours of torture.

Don't Invite a Sensitive Person for a Session at the Gym

Sensitive individuals love getting invites to catch up over lunch, a shopping spree or enjoying a leisurely stroll. However, they detest accepting an invite to accompany you to the gym. The idea of trying to talk and listen to someone while sweating it out on a treadmill is way too much for them to bear. Having others stare and move around them constantly will also irritate them. Yes, sensitive individuals find that exercise helps them relax, but only if it isn't too strenuous.

Allow Sensitive Individuals to Zone Out

Do not think that a sensitive individual who zones out in a public place is upset, bored, or trying to be annoying. A sensitive person has a huge amount of information to take in when in a public setting. All the smells, sound, and sights might, at times, be too much for them to bear. That is why they make use of a coping mechanism, for example, zoning out. That enables them to relax, take a deep breath and process everything around them. Thus, do not be bothered if your sensitive companion goes quiet within a moment's notice. Let them be quiet and deal with their surroundings the best way they know how.

Let Them Stare into Nothingness

Some people might find it rude; however, that is not the intention of sensitive individuals at all. Staring out into nothingness for a few minutes and then snapping back to reality helps them recuperate. Since sensitive individuals need to handle high amounts of concentration (which can overwhelm them easily), they need to take a few moments to sort through their thoughts before taking on the next set of thought. Thus, remember not to push them too hard as they might find the entire situation overwhelming and retreat to making use of their coping mechanisms.

Don't Retaliate at Their Criticism

Having a highly sensitive person as a friend or companion should be a huge blessing. Since these individuals are finely tuned to be aware of details non-sensitive individuals are not, they may advise you of something that needs improvement. With that said, there is no need to retaliate when they offer criticism as they are simply acknowledging the fact that they take note of fine details you might have otherwise missed. For example, if they taste a dish you have cooked and suggest you add additional spices, it might help improve the meal even more and even give you some ideas for your next meal as well. Thus, rather than be angry at them for correcting something, thank them for the criticism and use it to your advantage.

It's Normal for Sensitive People to Endure Days without Human Interaction

Since sensitive individuals do not have the need to interact with others a lot, do not panic if you don't see them for a couple of days. Sensitive individuals love spending time on their own and, apart from the occasional party or conversation, find peace in having a few quiet days to themselves.

Be Honest about Your Own Feelings

Sensitive individuals have their brain hardwired to sense if you feel happy, sad, or upset. Thus, if they ask you how you are feeling, do not brush it off as simply saying, "I am fine." These individuals will immediately sense that you are in fact not fine and their minds will kick into overdrive trying to figure out what how you really are feeling. This will be overwhelming for them and cause them to feel distracted. In turn, they will feel they might have let you down as they are not giving you the attention you deserve since something is clearly the matter. To prevent this scenario, rather be truthful about how you feel when they ask you.

Don't Push Your Political Opinions onto Sensitive Individuals

For a sensitive individual, political and issues regarding society might be overwhelming and worrisome. However, there is no need to avoid the subject completely. Be open with your sensitive companion and ask them if it would be all right to talk about these issues. Should they be okay with it, remember to never push your political views onto them. This will cause them to get angry, feel irritated and caged for a while after the conversation has ended.

Similar to the Above, Religion Is a Sensitive Subject as Well

It is never a good idea to expect a sensitive individual to believe what you believe in. Often, sensitive individuals are very passionate about their beliefs and find it very painful to have to think about something they do not believe in. Rather than wanting them to adhere to your beliefs, let them follow their own path leave them be.

Listening to the Listener

Sensitive individuals are keen listeners and will always be there when you need to get something off your chest. In return, when they have something to say, you need to listen to them as well. However, do not interrupt them while they are still talking. Instead, give them the attention they deserve and wait until they finish their story before you offer your advice. After all, sensitive individuals will sense when you are not listening to them,

Do Not Plan Their Day for Them

Some sensitive individuals will take their day by storm while others might take things slower. With that said, you should never tell your sensitive companion to pick up the pace or try to take things a little calmer. Let them plan their own day as they know how to take control of the amount of work they can handle in one go. Trying to get them to do more or less will only distract them from the task at hand, thus creating a rift in their already planned-out day.

Don't Think Sensitive People Are Judging

Sensitive individuals are in tune with others' emotions and will often make observations about it. That does not mean they are judging you. For them, it is just easier to not think about what others are thinking of them and rather focus on what they think about others. Since they observe others intensely, they will be very curious about certain groups of people. To sate their curiosity, instead of asking the group a huge number of questions, they will revert to books and online courses to learn more about people and their behaviors. Thus, don't find this judgmental; it's their way of learning more about you.

Don't Think You Need to Take Them for a Drink to Give Them a Good Time

Sensitive individuals prefer activities that involve art, movies, music, and creative sourcing. These activities don't always have to be outdoors and can be done in the comfort of their own home. With that said, don't think you need to take them out for a drink every time you want to show them what a good time feels like. They, in fact, prefer the less bustling side of life and would appreciate your gesture much more.

Tune Down the Music

Since sensitive people are very passionate when it comes to music, they might not like your music taste, and that is perfectly fine. You, on the other hand, might not like their music tastes either. But since you are in the company of a sensitive individual, there is no need to constantly blast out rock tunes when they detest that particular genre. Rather, settle for something you both like, and if they are open to it, they will learn to love your music on their own time—not when you blast it into their sensitive ears all day.

Clean up After Yourself

When living with a sensitive individual, you need to clean up after yourself. While this should be done even if your companion isn't sensitive, this can become simple excruciating for HSPs. Piles of clutter and messy environments irritate sensitive people a lot and might cause them to retaliate if the mess isn't cleared up. While they might clean it up themselves, you need to think of ways to ensure you clean up after yourself as well.

When It Comes to Working with Sensitive Individuals

Sensitive individuals focus really hard when they are busy with a particular task. When you interrupt them, it takes a while for them to regain focus after being distracted. This might overwhelm them as they might feel they are not completing the task to the best of their ability. To prevent this, rather converse about a certain time of day you would like to discuss something. That way, they won't lose focus, and they will give you their undivided attention once it is time to listen to what you'd like to discuss.

When They Take Something You Said or Did Personally

Have you ever told anyone, "You need to stop taking things personally all the time"? Chances are that person is a sensitive individual and deeply hurt by your comment. Since they are emotionally aware at all times, it is common for them to take something you said or did personally. Instead of judging them, learn why they acted up and perhaps do or say it differently next time.

Chapter 7

Living with a Sensitive Child

What's it like to parent a youngster whom others just "don't get"? Regularly sweet natured and anxious if it's not too much trouble, these are simple children to warm up to. They'll fascinate any individual who's around sufficiently long to observe their uncommon compassion for other people. In case you're feeling down, they can detect it, and their concern is significantly noticeable. It's hard not to be awed, as well, by their instinct, keen questions, and innovativeness—verification of a profoundly intelligent personality.

However, at that point, the clock strikes midnight. Something sets them off, and the impression of good development of "having everything in perfect order"—is abruptly cleared away. A huge emergency follows. Bystanders move back, puzzled.

The trigger could be one of numerous things: sand between the toes that is "excessively irritated," sudden cheering from the group that is "excessively terrifying," genial prodding that is "excessively frightful," or pressure from granddad to attempt a rope swing that is "excessively hazardous."

Guardians of these exceptionally sensitive children are acclimated with a look of bewilderment on the essences of relatives, companions and complete outsiders—a look that says, "Without a doubt, he can't be angry with that! What's up with him?" A few spectators make it one stride further, implying the guardians are at fault for being excessively liberal about their child.

It isn't so much that the analysis itself matters. What's alarming, for these guardians, is that the analysis underscores what a limited number of individuals understand their very sensitive youngster.

The Top Qualities of Sensitive Youngsters

High sensitivity has been concentrated in children and grown-ups for more than sixty years.

- They take in more tactile data from their condition than different children. Very sensitive kids hear sounds, identify unobtrusive scents and notice subtleties in illustrations and engineering that different children disregard. They may discover certain substances flavorful, or can't stand to wear certain clothing items.

- They process data at an alarming pace. Their imagination and instinct spring from this rich, profoundly intelligent inward-looking life.

- They have sharp compassion for other people. Exceptionally sensitive children go up against the feelings of everyone around them, partaking in their highs and lows.

- They are effectively overstimulated. Contrasted with other kids, sensitive children tire all the more quickly and need more rest or downtime.

- They are inclined to sudden fits of rage and emergencies, frequently accelerated by data overburden or passionate overburden. Circumstances intended to be a treat for a kid—an indoor play area, a birthday party or multi-day at an amusement park—can rapidly turn into a trial for sensitive children.

Taken together, exceptionally sensitive children see more, consider more and feel more.

The Three Most Important Factors to Take into Consideration When Dealing with a Very Sensitive Child

When quiet and cheerful, profoundly sensitive kids will, in general, stand out from the crowd, if simply because they don't participate. They watch the activity from the sidelines, are hesitant to talk up in class, and shun the weight of group activities.

These children are a long way from excited about new encounters: they like consistency. They stress during sleepovers, travels from home, the beginning of another school year, school field excursions, and social occasions—any of which may accelerate cerebral pains, stomach throbs, bad dreams or trouble eating or resting.

Of course, at that point, exceptionally sensitive youngsters are frequently named "modest," "on edge," or "moderate to adjust to change." Yet these marks don't decently mirror what's happening inside.

A Solid Feeling of Alertness

One of the logical models for the reason for sensitivity is that sensitive people have a functioning "conduct restraint framework." Some professionals consider this framework in the mind the "delay-to-check framework" since that is the thing that it truly does. It is intended to take a look at the circumstance you are in and check whether it is like any past circumstances put away in your memory.

Confronted with something new, a highly sensitive child needs to look at it, and whenever compelled to continue, may challenge, not appreciate it, or deny this "joy."

Keep in mind that any new experience implies a scary surge of new tactile encounters. Most HSCs appear to be poor connectors; however, as a general rule, they are being approached to adjust too excessively. They are overpowered, or scared of being overpowered, by all the new incitement that must be prepared before they can unwind.

A Sharp Consciousness of Potential Results

In light of their development and thinking abilities, an exceedingly sensitive youngster can envision the full effect of potential results, and they commonly overthink any situation. News reports of flames and break-ins will make them worry about the well-being in their own home. One of the greatest undertakings for a sensitive individual is to live bravely with full consciousness of the upsetting potential outcomes throughout everyday life. Highly sensitive children can't deny these just as others can.

Principles that Trips Them Up

Exceptionally sensitive kids are reliable. They need to "make the best decision" and take individual slip-ups more seriously than most. Being so "botch cognizant" makes them unsure. It's troublesome for them to disregard humiliation over "putting a foot wrong" out in the open. They don't think, "That just demonstrates I'm human"; they think, "That just demonstrates I'm lacking." Openly talking, music presentations, spelling bees, assignments, and tests can fill them with genuine fear to such an extent that they may perform under their capacity.

Taking Care of Your Highly Sensitive Child

Very sensitive youngsters are in danger of disguising, enduring, and profoundly harming feelings of disgrace—a feeling that they're some way or another "lacking" contrasted with all their other friends. Guardians and other grown-ups in their life need to do everything they can to keep this baseless feeling of disgrace from flourishing.

If you have a profoundly sensitive kid, the accompanying focuses are likely only updates for you. However, they might be useful for other people who are essential to your kid as well.

Accept Your Child

A very sensitive youngster's involvement of the world might be not quite the same as yours, yet it is genuine. The person in question isn't "faking" fits of rage or disappointment to get consideration or control you. Your youngster can't adjust to "resemble you" (in the event that you are not profoundly sensitive yourself), and the sooner you can acknowledge the kid you have, the more joyful you will both be. A key piece of tolerating your youngster is pinpointing every one of the things you like about an exceptionally sensitive disposition.

Show Your Child that You Approve

All exceptionally sensitive kids see that they are not quite the same as different children. Your youngster has to realize that you approve of them and that they are not a peculiarity. Advise them that numerous individuals resemble them.

When they face their shortcomings or failings, they need you to counter their self-questions with a progressively adjusted point of view. Raising triumph to coordinate a disappointment is critical for wiring your youngster's mind for confidence. Recognize the failure, yet advise them that they have other qualities where they have excelled in.

Give Your Child the Protection They Need

To manufacture trust in another circumstance, your exceptionally sensitive youngster should make littler strides than other kids, with bunches of support from you. Since a lot of your youngster's certainty is based on having had exceedingly positive encounters in the past that were comparable, it's critical not to compel your child to go past what they're all right with. Pushing this youngster to enable them "to get over their dread" will fail horribly. Don't give others a chance to force your youngster to accomplish something he isn't prepared to do.

Know That Your Child Will Be at Peace at a Slower Pace

Very sensitive children flourish with consistency and schedule, and they need significantly more downtime in their timetable than "normal" kids. Any exceptional experience ought to be adjusted by a calm, soothing "retreat" that enables them to regroup inwardly. After an errand with an adolescent, stop at home and have story time or shower time.

Plan some "moment withdraws" to anticipate overpower amid encounters that can't be interfered. An iPod with soft music, for instance, can give a quiet retreat to a youth amid a film in the theater. Enable more established children to withdraw to their room amid a supper party.

Have Patience with Your Child

With a very sensitive youngster, a basic excursion to the toy shop to pick a treat can take quite a while. These children need to contemplate choices and consider every one of their choices cautiously. Regardless of your disturbance in circumstances like this, you should be watchful how you show it. At the point when control's called for, recall that even a stern verbal railing can be pounding to these children. For the most part, they're unforgiving self-commentators, brisk to denounce themselves as "awful" or "pointless" when they mess up. It's a smart thought to finish up control with an update that everybody commits errors.

Remember that, at times, you will feel baffled that your life is compelled by every one of the things your youngster can't or won't do. And you will stress that your youngster's life is being constrained as well. Try not to worry pretty much all the "fun things" your youngster is by all accounts passing up. Your kid doesn't need to experience a similar youth that you did. The individual in question has their own thoughts regarding what is "entertaining." Remain positive, be glad for your youngster, and foresee an incredible future for them (which truly is well inside reach), and you'll help your youngster remain positive as well.

Help Them Understand Their Differences

This is probably one of the most important factors to take into consideration when taking care of your sensitive child. Since they are still growing and developing their own character, they are looking towards what other friends and family members are doing. A child tends to imitate what they see others do. Take, for example, a parent that tends to get violent when angry. The more the child gets exposed to such behavior, the more they will think it is acceptable to indulge in similar behavior.

With that said, a sensitive child who sees non-sensitive people act or speak in a particular way will start imitating this as well. However, since a sensitive child will react to certain situations differently than a non-sensitive child would, a barrier is instantly formed. The child might even question why his reaction wasn't the same as the person he was imitating. This causes confusion and will only add fuel to the fire.

However, as a caregiver to a sensitive child, it is your duty to help your child understand the most important differences between his reaction and that of others. Remember that youngsters might not always understand difficult phrases, thus it is recommended to be as subtle as possible. Help them understand that they are unique and have a very special gift. Do not let them see this as a curse as when they get older, they will resent the fact that they are highly sensitive.

Chapter 8

Being a Highly Sensitive Man

As an HSP, you need to learn to be your very own closest companion and make your prosperity a need. Nobody is going to totally understand why you turned down that social excursion following an animating day, or why you put your telephone on silent after 7:00 p.m.; however, you may be the special case who will get it.

As a man, masculinity is associated with your personality, and should you be a sensitive man, it might be hard to keep up that "tough" attitude. For that reason, many men feel downright weak when it comes to sensitivity. However, these sensitive attributes men have set them aside from the rest; they give them the ability to truly stay in tune with their companion.

If you are a highly sensitive man, you can make use of the following tips to ensure you don't overpower your very unique mind.

- Set aside an opportunity to yourself amid and after your day. It tends to finish a morning reflection, going out for a stroll without anyone else at lunch. It's tied in with setting aside a few minutes consistently to accomplish something quieting—alone.

- If you start to feel overpowered, take full breaths. Breathing affects the body and brain. It tends to be exceptionally useful in case you're amid an overstimulating action or condition and can't escape.

- Make a playlist of music that you find unwinding. Established music or instrumental jazz may work; however even acoustic covers or disengaged vocals of your main tunes may work.

- Start saying no. In the wake of a difficult day loaded up with responsibilities, it's not worth overpowering yourself with a solicitation to a noisy dance club or supper with companions. There's no motivation to feel regretful about it; you are dealing with yourself, so you can be taking care of business. Eventually, it benefits yourself as well as everybody around you.

- Make a protected, low-incitement space for yourself. This could be your room, your own office, or even a peaceful bistro you appreciate sitting in. Scarcely any things have a greater effect than having a spot you can go to so as to get away from the bustle.

- As exceptionally sensitive individuals, encounters can feel stupendously scary—and that is similarly as valid for men. Every sensation and feeling can be so unimaginably solid. Yet living as an HSP doesn't mean you need to be left overstimulated or overpowered. You can figure out how to deal with your daily practice and take advantage of your ground-breaking attribute.

Chapter 9

Growing up with Emotional Neglect

W hat does life entail when you grow up with emotional neglect? In order to answer this question, you first need to look at what emotional neglect as a child really entails:

- Guardians who said you were "being lousy" for having wild emotions.

- Your folks never communicated their very own feelings and were awkward when you did it.

- Being named a crybaby since you are too sensitive for their liking.

Unfortunately, this isn't unprecedented. Truth be told, research recommends that numerous families bring up their kids with emotional disregard—an inability to react to feelings. This can cause unfortunate results for any youngster, yet particularly, very sensitive youngsters. Emotional disregard can have as incredible an effect upon a kid as maltreatment, despite the fact that it's not discernible or critical as is mistreatment.

Understanding the Severity of Ignoring These Emotions

Emotional neglect takes place when a parent neglects to react to a youngster's passionate needs. Regularly, that absence of passionate reaction doesn't look unfortunate by any stretch of the imagination; the guardians may take extraordinary consideration of the youngster. Be that as it may, something undetectable is feeling the loss. The parent doesn't approve their youngster's sentiments or react to their passionate needs.

And that has results. Emotionally neglected kids can feel alone. As children, they feel like their needs aren't essential, that their sentiments don't make a difference or that they ought to never request help since it's an indication of shortcoming.

When adulthood rolls around, emotional neglect can become superfluous blame, self-outrage, fearlessness or a feeling of being defective. In any case, that is valid for any individual who grew up with emotional neglect. Imagine a scenario where you're an HSP. In the event that your being has made you very receptive to feelings, what does emotional neglect do to you?

Feelings are, from multiple points of view, an HSP's first language. And a careless family doesn't talk that language.

How Emotional Neglect Influences an Exceptionally Sensitive Youngster

Many researchers underline that you can't make a kid exceedingly sensitive with a passionate childhood and, on the other hand, you can't free somebody of being sensitive through emotional neglect. Sensitivity is a hereditary characteristic; either you're brought into the world with it, or you're not.

So emotional neglect doesn't change whether a kid is an HSP. However, it affects HSPs very uniquely in contrast to other youngsters.

While the guardians surely have feelings of their own, they abstain from communicating them apparently or recognizing the feelings of others. It resembles that they separate from themselves from the most essential piece of their HSP youngster's internal life.

Best case scenario, growing up as an HSP in a careless family resembles being an artist in a world with no melody. In different cases, it's much more awful. It's what could be compared to having guardians who disclose to you that your melody is awful.

Obviously, numerous HSPs don't need to envision that by any means; it's frequently how they were raised. And that sort of emotional neglect sends highly sensitive kids a clear message: Your most noteworthy quality isn't welcome here.

Different ways Emotional Neglect Damages Very Sensitive Youngsters

Everybody is influenced by their youth condition, regardless of whether it's great or terrible; however, for exceedingly sensitive individuals, this impact is intensified. Research recommends that HSPs endure more in awful conditions, however, do particularly well in great ones. So it's sensible to expect emotional neglect in youngsters will have a huge effect on them.

While only one out of every odd HSP youngster who manages emotional neglect will confront the majority of the circumstances beneath, a few results may include:

- Their high sensitivity becomes something to laugh at, even with their folks. Remarks that a youngster is "excessively sensitive" might be good-natured, however unavoidably seemed to be a negative judgment.

- Families may single out the HSP. Siblings are normally enduring emotional neglect as well, yet they may take normally to the "suck it up" message than their highly sensitive brother or sister. That makes it simple for them to set themselves at risk of being bullied or shunned.

- They believe there's a major issue with them. There's no restriction to how often we'll say it: Sensitive kids are as normal as any other child. Yet it's difficult to disguise that in case you're told again and again that you're the oddball. Rather, you disguise that your feelings aren't "right" and don't make a difference.

- Given the abovementioned, it's nothing unexpected that a sensitive youngster begins to underestimate themselves. In any case, careless guardians frequently consider this to be a frail spot, as well and weigh the kid to be progressively sure while never approving the youngster's qualities and emotions.

- Sensitive individuals respond unequivocally to analysis, and analysis is, in every case, hard for a kid. For an HSP youngster, emotional neglect implies that they never get the chance to see constructive and healthy emotional support. And, normally, they can't create a solid approach to manage analysis themselves if they never observe it demonstrated at home.

- All HSPs can move toward becoming overstimulated by boisterous or occupied conditions and overpowered by forceful feelings on occasion. In any case, HSPs figure out how to deal with this through self-care. Frequently they need a calm, safe spot to withdraw to. For very sensitive children, that is just conceivable if the parents understand this need. With that said, careless guardians are most certainly not. Rather, they consider it to be the youngster "going overboard." They may even get furious at the kid. This can make overpower the beginning of frenzy and dread in the youngster.

- At the point when a child's passionate needs don't make a difference and nobody appears to understand them, they retreat to keep themselves secluded. They may feel alone on the planet and, for a child, is almost unbearable.

- Any youngster who experiences emotional neglect discovers that they shouldn't request help since it won't be given or on the grounds that it seems "feeble." This is particularly harming to HSP kids since they have to figure out how to ask for necessities in a society that frequently doesn't understand them.

- Tension components can join to leave an HSP youngster with progressing uneasiness, powered by the dread that they are continually doing things "off-base."

When you start to regard yourself as though you matter, society will start to react to you in an unexpected way. They begin to see your identity, your feelings and what you feel is important.

Stages to Recuperating from Emotional Neglect as a Child

Emotional Neglect as a child doesn't vanish when you grow up. Grown-ups convey it with them into their lives, and it influences everything: their connections, their mental self-portrait, and their psychological prosperity.

However, emotional neglect is something you can recoup from. Here are a few ways to enable you to do that:

- Become acquainted with and acknowledge yourself. Remember to understand your high affectability as an essential advance toward tolerating your requirements as it is typical and legitimate. And finding out more about emotional neglect can enable you to recognize—and change—designs you're not mindful of.

- Acknowledge that your emotions and needs matter just like anybody else's. For an HSP, it may be accomplishing a greater amount of conversing when in the company of someone, voicing your necessities to other people or setting boundaries.

- Begin bringing life to your necessities. Individuals recuperating from emotional neglect regularly keep their feelings covered up on the grounds that their feelings are caged. As a highly sensitive person, that may mean you possibly express your necessities when you're totally overpowered or you pull back and never bring life to them. An opportunity to express your emotions should become part of your day-to-day life. When you start to regard yourself as though you matter, the general population in your life starts to see you in a more positive way and react to you in an unexpected way. They begin to see your identity, your feelings, and your needs. They also begin to react to what they can finally observe.

- Soothing oneself is a way the vast majority figures out how to do as children while being relieved by the grown-ups who adore them. In the event that you grew up with emotional neglect, you probably never taken in this ability, yet it's not difficult to adapt.

Chapter 10

What Does a Highly Sensitive Person Sense That Others Don't?

Since highly sensitive individuals have a gift that enables them to sense aromas, sounds, and emotions that otherwise would not have been noticeable. Let's have a look at some of the top senses that HSPs encounter.

Allergies

To better understand this scenario, let's look at an example where you, along with a colleague, stroll into the office together. Your colleague may begin wheezing, and you're completely fine. Odds are that the individuals from the cleaning team were careless with the cleaning chemicals and your buddy is having a serious response to the synthetic compounds.

Numerous HSPs just utilize characteristic cleaning items like lemon and vinegar since anything more grounded than that can make them have a sneezing fit.

Aromas

Have you, at any point, felt like you walked into a brick wall by somebody's aroma since they doused themselves in it, or that a few tones in the fragrance were simply overpowering? Envision encountering that numerous times each day, from all bearings and layered, so the fragrance of cooking gets mixed with the stench of a feline litter box, somebody's cologne, espresso—the list is endless. This can cause cerebral pains and sickness, particularly in confined spaces.

Sounds

If a rescue vehicle alarm sounds irritating to you, it very well may be an unbelievable torment to an HSP. Sharp, uproarious, and redundant sounds can feel like needles being crashed into their ears, and it's normal for them to get cerebral pain and totally lose the capacity to center for some time. Working or living in a zone where alarms moan all the time may bother a standard individual, however, can make an HSP crazy.

Likewise, repulsive to manage are sounds that other individuals don't hear, however, are angering for an HSP. The piercing whimper of an ice chest can break focus and shield an individual from resting or even reason uneasiness and a heightened heartbeat.

Layered Sounds

Numerous HSPs experience issues handling discernible data if they find themselves in a busy area. For instance: if a pack of individuals gets together in a swarmed bar and numerous individuals are talking at the same time while a television booms and music is playing, a highly sensitive individual can go into all-out tactile overpower and not have the capacity to perceive a solitary thing.

While you're having an incredible discussion, tuning in to a great song and blocking out the television talk, they won't be able to block a few things out and focus on others. It simply all comes in at an alarming rate, so they will be not able procedure anything you're stating.

Lights

Hardly anything can be as painful to a highly sensitive individual as a glinting fluorescent light, a strobe light, or an uncovered light. Delicate lights that fancy up a room is dazzling; however, sharp edges of light are difficult to see. They can't be overlooked; it is possible that they're excessively sharp and crash into a sensitive individual's eyes like when caught in a sandstorm.

Numerous HSPs will, likewise, turn down the light on PC screens, telephones, and iPads so they're not difficult to take a look at. If they don't do this, they might be in a constant condition of flinching in agony.

Tastes

If the fixings in an HSP's most-loved sustenance abruptly change, you can be sure they'll take note of it without a doubt. Regardless of whether this is on the grounds that they taste that their most-loved dish has begun to taste spicier or that the french fry shop is currently utilizing an alternate cooking oil, they'll be the first to notice.

They may even have inclinations for specific flavors such as maintaining a strategic distance from disgusting nourishments or sharp flavors and leaning toward substances that are consoling and calming.

73

Dramatic Weather Changes

A move in weather conditions can make an HSP feel blackout or sickened, and it's very regular for them to get headaches. Weather changes can, likewise, influence torment conditions like joint inflammation, so the highly sensitive person in your life might be crippled by an approaching snowstorm or substantial precipitation.

Air Contamination

Much the same as those synthetic cleaning substances drifting around, outside contamination will influence an HSP significantly more than another person. Since they're bound to have asthma, they're somewhat similar to keeping a canary on a coal mine site. If you put them outside, they might not be able to survive, since they'll be wheezing in a matter of moments.

Swarmed city avenues brimming with vehicle fumes may make them sick for quite a long time, which is the reason such a large number of HSPs discover harmony and comfort in rustic regions since they are significantly calm and tranquil as well as the air being breathable.

Sensitivity toward Food

It's normal for a highly sensitive individual to have nourishment hypersensitivities, and these can change as they experience life. Substances they adored as kids may set them off further down the road, or the other way around. Some may have the Celiac illness or Crohn's, or anaphylactic responses to everything from mushrooms and peanuts to garlic or celery.

In the event that an HSP just eats a little, controlled assortment of substances, they might be not able to eat anything else without getting savagely sick.

Immune System Conditions

By far, most individuals with immune system maladies or sensitivities are HSPs. They will, in general, be sick regularly and can experience the ill effects of everything from joint conditions to thyroid issues. A large number of their infirmities can be lightened with a calming diet which is intended to diminish irritation by killing allergens and activating nourishments.

Increased Feeling of Agony

Needles, stings, menstrual cramps, toothaches—these agonies may influence HSPs unquestionably more than others. Torment that registers as a two or three on a standard agony scale might be progressively similar to a five or six to an HSP. Moreover, it can frequently take an HSP longer to recoup from wounds or surgeries than other individuals.

Clothing Items

Small issues with your dress that may simply bother you for only a few seconds can be unbearable for an HSP. That "sort of bothersome" woolen sweater? No doubt, it feels like steel fleece and spiked metal ripping their skin from their bones. The tag attached to their clothes is crushing into their back and making them need to rip all their garments off and throw them away.

Pants feel like they're made of cardboard boxes, and their silk pullover is undulating and stroking them delicately, making their skin run hot and cold all at once. Numerous HSPs will shun what's trendy for what's agreeable and what they can really endure.

Chapter 11

Highly Sensitive Individuals and Depression

Since highly sensitive individuals lead such different lives from that of other people, it is common for them to fall into a spiral of depression. With that said, let's have a look at some of the main reasons highly sensitive individuals are more susceptible to depression.

Constant Natural Overstimulation

Unfortunately "leaving" an over-animating condition isn't always possible. A sensitive youngster may not leave a bustling classroom. A specialist may not generally have the advantage of leaving an unbearable work environment. An adoring, sensitive mother can't abandon her youngsters when they are "over-animating."

Research with animals has demonstrated that when a creature comes to trust that it can't escape a tormenting domain, it creates sentiments of "learned powerlessness" and winds up miserable and discouraged. Over-incitement is a horrendous, aversive affair for everybody.

HSPs who are constantly over-invigorated and feel unequipped for practicing authority over their condition might be at higher hazard for creating sentiments of vulnerability, misery and then sadness.

Awareness of Your Inner Self

HSPs are intent on checking out data and signs from their bodies. Vibes of yearning, thirst, overwarming, physical tiredness, inadequate rest; all are extremely convincing and obvious to them. Thus, HSPs occasionally worry a lot more about their well-being and may make pressing demands on their condition for consideration or backing.

This increased familiarity with their human helplessness may add to sentiments of uneasiness and a feeling of powerlessness which, again adds to the development of burdensome emotions.

A Rich and Invigorating Life

Should a HSP lead a rich and invigorating life, this individual might feel as if a set of unknown negative sentiments lie just a few feet away. This is where one's subconscious being comes into play as what seems to be a full and happy life is being bombarded with "what if's." These uncertainties lead to a sense of powerlessness and even miserable sorrow in some cases.

Relational Over-incitement

People are very invigorating to be near! Every single person is always flagging their passionate states to each other through a manner of speaking, stance, and signals. It is characteristically human to react empathically to these signs—to understand and "feel together" with people around us. HSPs with their permeable incitement hindrances are gifted and oblivious relational flag pursuers.

Accordingly, they are frequently caught by the conditions of everyone around them or even by the situation of individuals on the news or in anecdotal portrayals. They may encounter these resonances unequivocally.

In the event that an HSP is in an intimate relationship with a discouraged or sick individual, they may think that it is troublesome not to wind up discouraged themselves.

Burdening Reactions

Since HSPs are very sensitive to their bodies, they see the physical changes which happen in light of low dimensions of ecological contaminants or low portions of prescriptions. Symptoms which may be minor in others might be noticeable in sensitive people. A few drugs may have dejection as a symptom: Hypertension and cholesterol drugs can reason dejection indications as can a few meds for a cardiovascular ailment, in light of the fact that these prescriptions influence the cerebrum. Oral contraceptives and hormone substitution meds may also influence the state of mind—an endless loop. The convergence of these components may make a "flawless tempest" for some HSPs.

Sensitivity to their very own reactions prompts sentiments of delicacy which thus persuade the person that they can't change or impact their condition. On-edge discernment adds to the sentiment of defenselessness or sadness that prompts discouragement. Pollution by the sadness or uneasiness of others around them may add to their somber view.

Sensitive people are ready to appreciate pleasurable incitement and take advantage of the affection, backing, and enthusiasm of everyone around them.

HSPs also take advantage of psychotherapeutic help which causes them to re-outline their experience toward a positive and enabled viewpoint on themselves, their capacities and their capability to control their condition adequately.

Sensitivity is a piece of the typical range of human responsiveness. It comes with goodies in endowments of perceptiveness, instinct, scruples and sympathy for other people; characteristics which are of incalculable incentive to human culture.

Chapter 12

Highly Sensitive Individuals and Dipolar Disorder

Numerous HSPs are misdiagnosed as having psychological maladjustment, for example, ADHD, summed-up nervousness issue, social tension issue, discouragement, or bipolar issues. Be that as it may, sensitivity is not a dysfunctional behavior and being an HSP does not cause sadness, uneasiness issue, bipolar turmoil or some other psychological instability. Truth be told, HSPs have assets that assist in ensuring us against it. With a decent childhood, our characteristic can make us socially able, versatile and ready to appreciate life, much like a non-sensitive individual in a similar domain.

Be that as it may, numerous individuals with bipolar conditions are profoundly sensitive, so the difficulties that accompany high affectability can make adapting to their psychological sickness more troublesome, particularly when feelings of anxiety end up overpowering.

In the event that you are sensitive and have bipolar issues, the world can feel like a mind-boggling, overstimulating place from which there is no getaway. However, that doesn't mean you need to feel awful about your identity. There are ways to enable yourself to deal with your condition and your attribute as well as manage the stressors that influence you before they get you down.

What Is Bipolar Disorder?

Researchers portray bipolar issues as a psychological sickness that influences the synthetic substances in your mind and causes emotional episodes, shifting back and forth between times of despondency and craziness. This variation from the norm in mind science prompts challenges in controlling compelling feelings just as a wide assortment of other conceivable side effects including uneasiness, poor focus, the inability to sleep, and affectability to clamor.

Individuals with this issue can feel sad and miserable, bad-tempered, and furious, and experience the ill effects of low confidence, the absence of certainty, and feeling useless. In a condition of lunacy, they may feel euphoric, with a feeling of grandiosity, bringing about misguided thinking and high hazard practices, for example, drinking, betting, spending binges and unsafe sex, participating in such a large number of exercises and the failure to perceive their disease.

Another examination has uncovered that individuals with bipolar issues, around 60 million around the world, experience a diminishing of dark issues in areas of the cerebrum in charge of restraint and feeling, which proposes why they may experience issues controlling their sentiments and directing their conduct.

Why It Is Important to Acknowledge If You Are a Sensitive Person with Bipolar Issues

If you are exceedingly sensitive and bipolar, acknowledging and controlling it is vital. Both HSPs and individuals with bipolar issues progress toward becoming overpowered by clamor and other tangible incitement around them, which causes a great deal of pressure. This is the process in which the minds of both very sensitive individuals and those with bipolar issues have a decreased capacity to sift through change. At the end of the day, your mind lets in more data, making you both imaginative and effectively overpowered, which prompts a weakness to stretch. The more focused you are, the more probable you are to wind up discouraged, on edge, furious or hyper. Without managing your feelings of anxiety soundly, you're bound to fall back on undesirable adapting strategies, for example, utilizing medications or liquor, which makes you increasingly helpless against dysfunctional behavior.

Research has demonstrated that individuals with bipolar experience more unpleasant occasions than the normal individual. This hypothesis recommends that people with bipolar may produce their very own worry because of their contrary musings, side effects, and conduct, which may trigger burdensome indications. So it gives the idea that discouraged and bipolar people both create worry just as respond to it.

Individuals with bipolar confusion additionally have more trouble recouping from circumstances that reason pressure, so overseeing it every day is fundamental.

Adapting to Pressure

Stress influences your body, conduct, and considerations, and in the meantime, your body, conduct, and contemplations influence your feeling of anxiety. As somebody with bipolar confusion and an exceptionally sensitive individual, you will be worried by regular daily existence, so it's imperative to perceive what focuses or overpowers you. These might be things that may not trouble other individuals. Try not to reprimand yourself for your emotions. Rather, deal with your feelings of anxiety by perceiving what triggers worry for you.

Here are ways you can calm your feelings if you have bipolar issues and you are a sensitive person.

- Individuals with bipolar frequently have a misshaped view of the real world, so they may misunderstand and misread others' words and articulations and arrive at false resolutions. The more you can converse with your companions, friends, and family about your recognition, responses, and encounters, the more beneficial your connections will be. Tell individuals what you need, regardless of whether it's a great opportunity to be distant from everyone else, to unwind or to talk. Nobody can peruse your brain, and it's dependent upon you to impart so you get what you need.

- Realize what triggers worry for you and how that influences your dispositions. By creating mindfulness, you can keep away from those stressors and perceive the standpoint of your disposition to change so you can make a move to control them.

- When you see that you're feeling on edge, furious or upset, you can figure out how to perceive your body responding to those sentiments. When you do, unwinding methods like contemplation, exercise, back rubs, and deep breathing can quiet both your body and your psyche. Individuals with bipolar may also profit by medicine, so address your specialist about getting the correct drug for you.

- Stress can lead a few people to unhelpful conduct, which causes more pressure, harms connections and can trigger a descending winding into sorrow. Such conduct may incorporate going out, investing too much energy alone and ruminating, drinking, taking medications, betting or overspending. Attempt to slow down if you're trying too hard and make a stride back to reassess.

- Change your reasoning. You can change unhelpful contemplations by changing the substance of what you're considering and concentrating on the real world. See how undermining a stressor truly is. You can change your reasoning procedure by concentrating on a solid movement, for example, cooking or planting as opposed to ruminating about what's focusing on you.

- Low confidence and sentiments of deficiency or disgrace that can result from long stretches of being misconstrued and scrutinized can make both HSPs and individuals with bipolar vulnerable to sinking into burdensome states. Sensitivity itself does not cause wretchedness or uneasiness, yet the negative emotions about yourself can make you defenseless against it. Scientists contemplating the connection between the two found that sorrow did not prompt low confidence; however, individuals with low confidence are inclined to concentrating on negative musings, putting them in danger of misery. So managing your sentiments might be the most imperative advance toward counteractive action and the board of your psychological wellness.

- To enhance your confidence, have a look at when you are saying negative things regarding yourself, both in your considerations and the words you express and let them go. Specialists in this field recommend focusing on your requirement for endorsement. Individuals with low confidence will, in general, look for methods for demonstrating their contrary convictions about themselves, so they will look for endorsement and partner with individuals who affirm their negative mental self-view, which just exacerbates them about how they feel about themselves.

Individuals with bipolar can feel like they have no power over their states of mind, conduct, and sentiments, which can make them feel disappointed, restless and lead to burdensome manifestations. Numerous sensitive individuals feel similar. However, accusing yourself and feeling awful about your identity or falling back on damaging conduct as a departure will just exacerbate how you feel and potentially trigger further pressure and burdensome indications.

If you are both very sensitive and bipolar, you have to deal with yourself, beginning with your convictions about yourself. Try not to trust negative considerations and words, regardless of whether they're spoken by you or any other person. You have unexpected needs in comparison to other individuals. Begin by being proactive and assuming the responsibility of your own self-care to support your certainty. And the more mindful you wind up about what stresses you, how stress influences you and what you have to ease it, the more benefits you will have.

Chapter 13

Highly Sensitive Individuals and the Loss of a Pet

Having a pet is something not all individuals indulge in; however, many feel the need to have a companion to keep them company at all times. Thus, when you pour your heart and soul into loving and caring for a pet and the pet dies, it is natural to feel sad and grieve. However, for a highly sensitive person, this process goes along with severe emotional trauma. For HSPs, it is necessary to make use of the following steps to deal with this trauma.

Allow Yourself to Mourn

At the point when an adored pet dies, it's totally normal to feel overpowered by the profundity of your anguish. Amid this time, it's critical to give yourself the authorization to mourn. You may find that it happens in stages, where sentiments, for example, stun, forswearing, outrage, blame, dejection, and gloom come in turns. Or on the other hand, you may experience your misery in waves, a progression of highs and lows.

Distress tends to make you easily affected—the exact opposite thing a very sensitive individual needs. At the point when distress assumes control, it will appear as though the entirety of your emotions has been amplified. You will feel them so strongly that, on occasion, it might appear as though your body can't handle the torment. Yet it can, and you will almost certainly live and feel whole once more.

The lamenting procedure happens continuously and can't be constrained or rushed. You may begin to feel better in months, or it might take years. Whatever your experience, it's important to be understanding with yourself and go at your own pace.

Don't Blame Yourself

The vast majority of us trust that our pets will pass calmly in their rest. Sadly, it rarely happens that way. One of the hardest parts of thinking about a pet is confronting the likelihood of killing. Despite the fact that willful extermination frequently saves our pets from the agony and enduring of the end phases of life, many pet proprietors feel blame at settling on that decision for their valuable sidekick.

These sentiments of blame regularly focus on stresses that the choice to euthanize was untimely, or on the other hand, that it was past due. Some pet proprietors may even mark themselves a killer, allocating the blame of the misfortune to themselves rather than the sickness or occasion that really ended the life of their pet. As agonizing as willful extermination is for us, know that it tends to be a blessing we can provide for our pets; an approach to state thank you for all the solace and satisfaction they offered us by consummation their enduring in a noble, easy, and cherishing way.

Don't Put up a Wall around Your Emotions

In case you're an exceedingly sensitive individual who pulls back when harmed, you may wind up separated in your sadness. Tragically, in the event that you keep on conveying that torment alone, you won't recuperate. As unimaginable as it might appear, it's vital to connect with a companion or relative. Try not to stress over troubling another person with your anguish; the general population who adore you need to help. In the event that your jobs were turned around, you realize you would need your friends and family to come to you if they required a comforting presence.

Adapt to the New Chapter

In case you're searching for solid approaches to adapt to the torment of your misfortune and deal with your pain, think about the following:

- Lyrics, papers, short stories, and articles are a great way to adapt to your misery through the composed word.

- Respect your pet by planting a tree, making a gift to someone or assembling a scrapbook.

- Connect with loved ones to hold a dedication administration. You can bid a fond farewell and commend your pet's existence with your loved ones.

- You may stall and battle to open up to friends and family. If you wish, you can even search for hotlines that will be able to give you the support you need to process the death of your beloved pet.

- Killing and incidental passing can add an awful part to despondency and misfortune. Side effects of PTSD can meddle with your everyday working. In the event that you have these side effects and they hold on over weeks or months; it may be an ideal opportunity to converse with a professional. Examining your sentiments can help ease self-question and ruinous propensities.

Take Care of Yourself

The strain of losing a pet can debilitate your vitality, which can make it difficult to deal with yourself. Do what you can to guarantee you're getting the sustenance, exercise and rest you need. Invest a lot of valuable energy with the general population who care about you.

Take a break if you feel too diverted to even consider doing your daily activities right. Try not to be reluctant to take a three day weekend since you're stressed over what your supervisor will think or would prefer not to be viewed as replaceable. Dealing with your psychological well-being will improve you a representative over the long haul.

Losing a pet is one of the hardest things you'll ever experience, and the agony of that misfortune will be unendurable at first. However, over the long haul, the force of these emotions will vanish. Realize that there will come a few days when you can think back on affectionate recollections of your companion with both love and a solid heart.

Chapter 14

Why It Is Hard for an HSP to Travel

Travel should be something to be enjoyed. It should be a "get away from" opportunity to re-examine yourself. However, when you're an exceptionally sensitive individual, travel is the inverse: one major stress and overpower.

There are valid justifications for this, and it's not something you have to pummel yourself over. For sensitives, travel accompanies various traps. Let's investigate why travel can be intense for HSPs, and how they can begin appreciating it more.

The most compelling motivation travel can be troublesome for HSPs is that it hauls them out of their everyday practice. Routine is a comfort for sensitive spirits since it's the one thing that is steady and consoling in a bustling world. Losing that, even briefly, can be more intense for HSPs than it is for other people.

Most HSPs dislike being tossed into another condition, encompassed by new sights, sounds, nourishments, and circumstances and held to a schedule that they can't generally control. Individuals bear little challenges to travel, sensitive or not, like being packed into a minor plane seat or racing to make a corresponding flight. In any case, an exceptionally sensitive individual's framework forms everything all the more profoundly, amplifying these ordinary worries into totally nerve-wracking circumstances.

Numerous HSPs have discovered approaches to make travel less overpowering, even a little delightful.

The Most Effective Method to Appreciate Travel as an Exceptionally Sensitive Individual

Oppose the Strain to Continue Working

It appears as though every time sensitives go on an excursion, there's an extensive rundown of stuff they "have" to do. Things to see, things to encounter, even things to eat. If you just have a couple of days to go someplace astonishing, don't you need to see everything?

That is the way to simply going into disrepair and smashing. An excessive number of exercises wear sensitives out, make them grouchy and undesirable to be near.

Some portion of the reason it's so natural to get worn out on an excursion is on the grounds that sensitives become tied up with the possibility that we need to see "everything." However, you can never observe or do everything in another area, regardless of whether you have an entire week or two.

Rather, grasp the way that, as a profoundly sensitive individual, travel doesn't mean a similar thing to you that it intends to other individuals. You can investigate at your own pace. You can have a little experience and at that point call it enough. It helps to remember that before you go, you're making a schedule.

If you prefer to be on the shoreline over snorkeling on a coral reef, do that and let your friends know. In case you're doing it yourself, they'll acknowledge it as well, and they'll go about doing their own thing.

Build up a Daily Schedule

For sensitives, traveling shakes up your work routine, your home life, your financial plan and the greater part of all, your feeling of what's in store. So it's nothing unexpected that, despite the fact that numerous individuals love to travel, it's additionally a standout amongst the most distressing things that an HSP can manage.

A simple way to manage your traveling days is making use of the following example:

- Mondays are travel days. Early flights and transports are favored so you can do grocery shopping after you arrive.

- Tuesdays are easy-going touring days without any commitments and an opportunity to revive.

- Wednesdays and Thursdays are for working.

- Fridays and end of the week switch back and forth between trips and self-improvement exercises like taking a yoga class.

A large portion of us aren't jet-setters and don't have that dimension of adaptability. In the event that you keep your schedule similar to each time you go, it may be much less demanding to modify. For instance, your timetable could be:

- Day one is for remaining close to the inn, resting, and investigating the close-by neighborhood.

- Day two is for the "huge energizing movement."

- Day three is for social exercises like historical scenes.

You get the thought. Change to meet your very own requirements; however, if you set a schedule, you won't overpower yourself.

Have a Day Off

An off day is an entire day you take at home after the outing is finished, where you're only recuperating. What that implies will rely upon the individual. A day off means that you're unloading, tidying up, and getting some R&R. For other people, it will mean you're investing energy with the children or arranging out your work week.

Consider it a need. Each voyager feels cleaned in the wake of returning home from an excursion, and for profoundly sensitive individuals, that inclination is amplified.

The best way to get your off day is to plan it. It won't simply occur, so this is an ideal opportunity to be your very own HSP advocate. In case you're flying home on a Sunday, utilize an excursion day to take Monday off. In case you're a stay-at-home parent, chat with your companion when arranging the trek and clarify why you need that additional day.

You can go on mysterious, extraordinary treks. However, the exceptionally sensitive adaptation of "mysterious" maybe not quite the same as another person's "otherworldly." And it requires a lot of downtime. That won't generally coordinate other individuals' concept of an excursion; however, what could be superior to anything a trek that is really unwinding?

Chapter 15

Best Careers for HSPs

When you hear "vocation," what emotions ring a bell? Do you consider accomplishing something you would prefer truly not to do, just to acquire a check? Do you picture tyrannical supervisors and a heartless spotlight on efficiency? In case you're a very sensitive individual, there's a decent shot that work is certifiably not a delightful piece of your life.

Obviously, very sensitive individuals aren't the main ones who worry over securing the correct position. Yet HSPs face obstructions that numerous different laborers don't. Some portion of being exceptionally sensitive is that you're inclined to overpower, you may battle with hurried due dates, and you're especially sensitive to basic working environment stressors, including the identities of those you need to work with. In particular, very sensitive individuals look for significance in their work and genuinely aren't getting it done without it.

And very frequently, the business world basically isn't set up to oblige or even show worry about these requirements.

In any case, that doesn't imply that each activity must be like this. Truth be told, there are ways that work great for the sensitive among us; particularly if you know your very own qualities.

Let's have a look at why sensitive individuals are so frequently despondent at work, and how they can manufacture a vocation that really brings them meaning.

HSPs Need a Vocation That Is Something beyond a Check

Occupation fulfillment is elusive regardless of your identity. It tends to be more difficult for exceptionally sensitive individuals, who for the most part need to feel some feeling of importance and reason in their work.

There's a valid justification HSPs feel this way. As an HSP, a day at work includes something other than carrying out the responsibility itself. It additionally implies the following:

- Monitoring and frequently dealing with the feelings of every other person you work with

- Sensing all the unobtrusive sounds, fragrances, and subtleties that a great many people see as a foundation

- Preparing all aspects of your day and giving it a greater amount of your psychological vitality than other individuals would

At the end of the day, work can be definitely more depleting for exceptionally sensitive individuals than it is for other people. Indeed, even at best, you might be overstimulated and out of vitality when you return home. It's no big surprise HSPs need their business to be significant: It may be the main thing they get the chance to do generally days.

Tragically, important employment can be especially elusive. Somewhat, this is only the idea of the economy; our advanced lifestyle demands a specific measure of tedious work, and its majority is at last drive by benefit, not mission. Even fields that are viewed as inventive or "important" like not-for-profit work, some random activity could scratch that tingle; the identities of those you work with play similarly as large a job in your activity fulfillment as the work itself.

That doesn't imply that getting a significant line of work is a result of pure chance; however, there are ways you can figure out how to maintain a strategic distance from. They include the following:

- Any occupations that are centered around deals or hitting numbers, particularly if they don't specifically address your very own qualities

- Occupations that will, naturally, incorporate a great deal of showdown

- Any activity where the workplace is by all accounts boisterous, wild or disorganized

Work that is centered around "exposure" with other individuals regardless of whether it's clients or relentless shared work with partners. HSPs are good with individuals; however, they need private time to process and do their best work.

Researchers caution that your collaborators and workplace will represent the moment of truth your feeling of joy at an occupation.

Indeed, even in your fantasy vocation field, you'll get a handle on consumed in case you're managing a discourteous, forceful supervisor consistently or an upsetting office dynamic.

The Best Vocations for Very Sensitive Individuals

Profoundly sensitive individuals have a great deal of qualities as representatives. Indeed, they give interesting abilities that numerous different laborers don't have. For instance, HSPs are strong and urging to everyone around them. They tune in to other people, focus on subtleties and set aside the opportunity to think things through before racing without hesitation. As pioneers, they put an extraordinary accentuation on building accord, which encourages them to assemble amazingly fit, faithful groups. And in all settings, they get on unpretentious subtlety and have an instinctive sense for how to manage individuals.

These qualities make an amazing aide for what sorts of vocations HSPs will appreciate the most and flourish in. With that said, the following are some of the best choices for a sensitive individual looking for a vocation.

Caretaker Roles

This general class incorporates vocations, for example, medical caretakers, specialists, and physical advisors, social laborers, psychotherapists, and individual mentors. These fields play to HSP qualities, including sympathy, empathy and instinctive familiarity with others' needs. Obviously, you'll manage a great deal of feelings from other individuals; however, HSPs are attracted to these fields and regularly discover them incredibly satisfying.

Inventive Expert

This incorporates jobs, for example, visual originators, publicists, illustrators, motion picture fashion designers, or any individual who gives their creative abilities something to do as normal everyday employment. These callings can be a pleasant method to construct proficient experience and acquire cash while building up your abilities as a craftsman. As a reward, these occupations will, in general, be exceptionally simple to do on an independent premise, which gives HSPs the adaptability and self-sufficiency they need in their calendars.

Church

Numerous HSPs consider their convictions more important than everyone around them. That enables them to be liberal and provide support. This makes for a powerful blend in any priest. Obviously, HSPs will be more natural than stubborn about their gifts and may need to endure a specific measure of structure to fill in as a spiritual guide.

The Scholarly Community

The scholarly world can be focused, yet it moves at an insightful pace that permits HSPs to utilize their qualities. You get the chance to invest some portion of your energy doing cautious, centered work where profound bits of knowledge are used. You also get the chance to invest energy educating and helping understudies, yet just for a certain part of your day. In particular, you get the opportunity to do important business related to a point you really care about.

Entrepreneur

As a representative, numerous HSPs feel unreasonably ignored for advancements, as though they aren't "administration material." Yet that is essentially false. An HSP can be groundbreakingly powerful as the leader of an organization. Huge numbers of the best private ventures, for example, boutiques, displays, and cafés can prosper when headed by a sensitive individual. An HSP will make an inviting, quieting climate; structure a space that really stands out; and manufacture a reliable group of staff who make the most of their occupations and like helping clients. In the event that you have a dream for a business, it's a decent approach.

Non-benefit Organizations

This one accompanies a major admonition: Non-benefit work can be similarly as upsetting as private division work. Numerous non-benefits aren't too sorted out as customary organizations and some utilization their great mission to legitimize low wages. In any case, don't give that a chance to hinder you. There are a number of non-benefits where the way of life is solid, helpful, and concentrated on really making a difference. Non-benefit callings that are particularly useful for HSPs incorporate managerial jobs, official chief, and advertising, as well as enrollment administrators.

IT Proficiencies

Coding is an imaginative procedure and one that is best done by somebody with an eye for detail and solid instinct. That implies that HSPs have an unmistakable edge as a product engineer, site designer, or in any job that requires education. Numerous innovation employments sport a progressively loosened-up work climate and an emphasis on remote work, which additionally helps for very sensitive individuals.

These are the best picks; however, they're only a beginning stage. As a very sensitive individual, the most ideal approach to get an important line of work is to consider your very own qualities and begin from that point and give careful consideration to the way of life of a work environment before making a decision.

Chapter 16

Top Nutrients for
Highly Sensitive Individuals

Researchers are very keen to share with you their top supplements and nutrient that they absolutely recommend for anybody who's highly stressed, who can't relax or consider themselves highly sensitive.

Being a highly sensitive person, you experience stress that is difficult to explain to people who do not see themselves as being highly sensitive. You seem to need a lot more time to repair, and you tend to get overwhelmed easily. You need more time to relax, to meditate and to be by yourself to function optimally. You need to take care of yourself, and that means fully accepting that you might have limits that aren't like everybody else's.

Some people really struggle to make the distinction between physical stress and energetic stress. So whenever you need to put on a show and you need to be extra energetic, vibrant, or extra sociable, that actually stresses you out. And yes, sometimes you do hide from the outside world especially since you've just had enough and nobody seems to understand.

Magnesium

Magnesium is required for over three hundred body reactions. The reason magnesium is really important for highly sensitive people is that every time you're stressed out, you make use of magnesium. Magnesium is a relaxant, and highly sensitive people may not be aware of all the muscular tension they're carrying around and how uptight they physically feel at the end of the day. Magnesium is really great for muscle cramps, twitches anxiety, depression, and irritability. Not only is magnesium going to help your body to relax when your body's relaxed, but your mind will also follow.

Epsom Salt

Epsom salt baths, which are a source of magnesium sulfate, also helps soothe a sensitive individual. This is a supplement for highly sensitive people to help them nourish the nervous system. Every time you stressed out of body uses these nutrients to help you cope physiologically, so conflict is absolutely essential for anybody who's stressed out, who's anxious, who are depressed, who's irritable. B-complex is a basic necessity to support your nervous system, your cardiovascular system and it's also essential for your metabolism to help you digest fats, proteins, and carbohydrates. A lot of you are competitors. So you tend to turn to food whenever you're highly stressed, and food nourishes you. But unfortunately, you oftentimes turn to high-calorie foods and low-nutrient foods which in the long term is going to deplete a mineral and vitamin status even further. So the supplements such as B-complex and magnesium can also help you reduce cravings.

Valerian

The one herb most sensitive individuals can't live without in the first-aid department is Valerian. You can go to your local health food store and buy a small bottle of tincture, or you can even try tablets. Valerian is a sedative and a relaxant, and it just buffers out your ability and hypersensitivity. All you need to do is take a teaspoon dissolved in half a glass of water if you had a really overstimulating stressful day and your mind is buzzing and you can't sleep. Valerian is really great for nurturing and nourishing the nervous system. If you know that you're going to have a busy day, you might take a dose of delirium first thing in the morning just to help you ease through the day.

Vitamin C

For anybody who's experiencing a lot of stress is vitamin C. Vitamin C is absolutely essential for healing repair, immune system function. If you're really stressed out, your immune system drops, you tend to catch colds and flu a lot more and there's definitely a strong link between immunity and stress. We actually use Vitamin C at a significantly faster pace if we're stressed out.

What a normal person considers a moderate level of stress we consider a huge amount of stress so if you're feeling rundown and you feel that you're catching because you've been in a really stressful environment for too long definitely up your body. If you're finding that you can't recover from things bottoming out, you need to top up on the vitamin C.

Rescue Remedy

Rescue remedy can be considered as an energetic medicine. This remedy consists of a number of flower essences that help us deal with almost all stressful situations. The essences in Rescue Remedy can help with panic and irritation in patients in attentiveness lack of focus, risky remedies, fantastic at relieving anxiety, stress, any shock or even if you can see that situation traumatic.

Chapter 17

Highly Sensitive Individuals and Exercise

Everyone should indulge in some sort of bodily movement, but for sensitive individuals, it is even more important to engage in some form of exercise.

Exercise helps with the following:

- Enhanced rest

- Expanded enthusiasm for sex

- Better continuance

- Stress alleviation

- Perking up

- Expanded vitality and stamina

- Decreased tiredness that can increment mental readiness

- Weight decrease

- Diminished cholesterol and enhanced cardiovascular wellness

Building up a decent exercise plan can be somewhat testing as a profoundly sensitive individual. Not on the grounds that they need "extraordinary" activities or voodoo enchantment. But since the conditions encompassing that activity may be conditioned down an indent from the cliché styles in which we have come to know it.

Preparing Your Exercise Routine

This isn't only for powerlifting men at the wellness club. Everybody ought to take part in some type of solidarity exercise routines. That will practically keep any rock standing which you may have dreaded would fall.

The test with routines for profoundly sensitive individuals is that many people expect it must be done for a few hours a day. It's not just the hours that are the issue but instead that it requires stepping on weight machines in centers that will draw in alpha style center rodents into the scene. So for a very sensitive individual, you should think about acquiring some free gym videos for your home. A straightforward net search for "modest weight set" yields a huge amount of results. In the event that you need assistance recognizing how to manage those free videos, you can generally:

- Discover prerecorded videos to follow in the comfort of your own home.

- Download applications that assist you through videos.

- Think about working with a fitness coach. That guarantees that you have better structure and it will advance a close association with another individual.

Cardio Exercise

This is critical for consuming fat and for keeping that heart muscles solid. It's accommodating for very sensitive individuals since it helps consume overabundance cortisol and encourages endorphins. Given that exceptionally sensitive individuals are increasingly inclined to be influenced by negative pressure, practice is a standout amongst the most useful assets they can have. It flushes out the strain and replaces it with a feeling of solidarity and establishment.

However, not all HSPs are excited with jumping onto a complex cardio machine. You don't need to consider where you're going on a machine. Others, however, consider it to be a celebrated hamster wheel. And those wellness classes? Some HSP love the association they feel in a gathering; however, others loathe the foolishly uproarious music and odd chirpy educators.

So here are a couple of thoughts to consider:

- Most HSPs love getting out in nature. It's a standout amongst the most renewing acts you can take part in. What better drug, along these lines, than a climb in the slopes? Or on the other hand a stroll in the fields? What are some calm open-air spaces close to you that you may investigate?

- If you need to join a class but don't need the extreme clamor and mental mess that accompanies a high-vitality gathering, you can partake a cardio-yoga class. That way, you can get similar advantages without feeling overpowered.

- If you feel more secure at home and in isolation, take a stab at online editions. There are incalculable applications accessible to enable you to get a decent cardio exercise.

- Figure out how to connect cardio with different things you appreciate doing.

Yoga

This is a great method to incorporate adaptability into a bigger exercise schedule. It assists with portability, but since such a significant number of the stances in yoga classes require parity and quality, it can enable you to lessen your opportunity of damage while taking part in different activities as well. You can join classes if you feel good. If not, you can attempt online yoga classes as well.

Here's something important to remember: when endeavoring to heat up, you are best served by doing dynamic stretches, not dormant ones. In a perfect world, the stretches you do will impersonate components of the developments you will do in your exercise.

Subsequent to working out, that is the point at which those stale stretches will serve you better. The ideal approach is to extend the muscle for fifteen to thirty seconds. However, which muscles would be advisable for you to extend? A few specialists state you should extend everything. Others express it's smarter to stretch only a few. Others feel the need to cling to the approach of extending whatever feels hardened. If you think you have to stretch; proceed! No one should be narrow-minded about it.

Exercise is useful for everybody. Not simply very sensitive individuals. By all accounts, exercise is especially useful for those with increasingly sensitive sensory systems. It encourages them to consume off the abundance of stress and gets a hit of the vibe of great hormones, and it even assists with rest. And as all exceptionally sensitive individuals know, if you can get a decent night's rest, you can do pretty much anything.

With all this in mind, yoga is a great way of finding inner-peace and as a sensitive person; it's fantastic to combine a workout with finding peace. Yoga exercises the mind as well as the body to "think as one" and open a channel to positivity – something every sensitive individual strives for.

Chapter 18

Having a Look at the Confessions of HSP

One of the best ways of connecting with highly sensitive individuals or relating to other highly sensitive spirits such as yourself, it's always a good idea to have a look at confessions of HSP. Below are a number of confessions, and if you are an HSP, you might even relate to one or more of them.

I Truly Love Being on My Own

I cherish my loved ones, yet being distant from everyone else feels so great. Being separated from everyone else implies doing the things that truly matter to me, and that places me in a condition of profound focus and stream. It implies getting the chance to have things my way, without considering other individuals. I don't require other individuals to engage with me, and the sort of things that the vast majority do to mingle don't intrigue me much.

I Don't Find Everything That Goes on in Discussions Significant

I'm generally not so keen on what commonly goes for discussion. Making casual discussion just to be well mannered feels forced, despite the fact that I regularly end up doing it since it's anticipated from me. I'd preferably have one snapshot of association with somebody over a thousand immaterial ones.

Odds are that in the event that you request that I hang out a minute ago, I'll come up with a rationalization not to go, regardless of whether I don't have anything else going on. My psyche is normally making arrangements. In the event that I intended to remain home and "do nothing," at that point that is what I'm eager to do. If very late get-together comes up, I experience difficulty changing gears and making headspace for this new thought regardless of whether it's something I may appreciate.

I Lie to Escape Social Circumstances

I realize I ought to take the high ground and clarify that I'm a loner who gets depleted by mingling; however, I frequently don't do that. Yet on different occasions, similar to when you welcome me to your birthday bar at the end of the week that includes many associates I may not know, I'm just reasoning about not offending you and how I can keep up a decent working association with you. So I state I have other obligation, regardless of whether I don't.

I Get So Overpowered with Clamor and Individuals That I Cry

A week ago, following a seven-day getaway that included loads of associating with individuals I didn't know and investing a great deal of energy in overstimulating conditions, I burst into tears in a coffeehouse.

There is So Much Going on in My Mind I Feel Crazy

I have those profound self-observer considerations about existing on different planets and the conflicting idea of mankind. Be that as it may, once in a while my superpower of deep thinking goes excessively far. I invest hours on a contention I had with my life partner, thinking of new and better replies. I stall on one unimportant detail, for example, regardless of whether I should pack a lightweight sweater or a general-use coat for my up and coming excursion.

I Just Like a Handful of Individuals

I have a little group of friends to a limited extent since I'm a contemplative person who likes it as such, yet in addition since I don't meet many individuals who I click with.

I Have a Feeling That I'm Faking It When I Meet New Individuals

Utilize your "noisy" voice. Get some information about the people you will be interacting with. There are numerous ways I've learned to seem progressively social. "Peopling" will never feel totally normal to me.

I'm Superior to My Early Introduction

An outgoing companion once revealed to me she thought I was "a bitch" when she initially met me since I was tranquil. I wasn't endeavoring to be inconsiderate. I simply keep quiet around individuals I don't know well. It requires investment for me to feel good enough to give my genuine identity a chance to shine.

A Ton of Discussions Move Too Rapidly for My Contemplative Mind to Keep Up

Thoughtful people will, in general, need time to think before talking. My mind feels like it's running on high while every other people are tranquil.

I'm Awful at Indicating How I Feel

A manager once disclosed to me she thought I needed "enthusiasm" for a vocation I was amped up for. Men I've loved or dated had no clue that I was into them. I will keep my sentiments my own. It simply doesn't jump out at me to give them a chance to shine.

At Times I Wish I Could Vanish

By this, I mean to desert every one of my commitments, to turn off my telephone, and to locate a peaceful corner of the world to peruse and eat chocolate alone. Yet just for a brief period.

I am an Expert in Being Distant from Everyone Else

I need love, brotherhood, and soul-associations as well. The issue is these important connections are elusive. The vast majority of mingling is simply not enough.

I Quietly Cheer Each Time My Partner Has Plans

We're the two loners, so we end up at home a ton of the time. We live in a one-room condo, which doesn't leave us with a ton of room to get away from one another. When he leaves for his weekly gaming gathering or the intermittent supper with a companion, I'm in self-observer paradise.

I Suck at Staying in Contact

To everyone in my life, I really, profoundly, frantically cherish you. You are the people who influence my reality to go round. I'm sad to say I'm so awful at grabbing the telephone and messaging or calling. I become mixed up in my own little contemplative world some of the time.

Chapter 19

Debunking the Myths of
Highly Sensitive Individuals

Many sensitive individuals find it hard to put a voice to some of the myths the general population believes about their behaviors. Below is a list of debunked myths that clear the air between the general population and sensitive individuals.

It's only thoughtful people who are exceptionally sensitive.

That's false. Numerous loners are exceedingly sensitive, yet around 30 percent of exceptionally sensitive individuals are outgoing individuals.

Very Sensitive Individuals Are Timid

Some are bashful; however, some are most certainly not. Bashfulness is the devastating apprehension of a negative judgment in social circumstances, while high affectability is monitoring nuances and being overpowered when in an exceptionally invigorating condition. Very sensitive individuals may seem hindered on the grounds that they're mindful of the considerable number of potential outcomes in particular circumstances. They may delay before acting and about their past encounters.

Most Exceptionally Sensitive Individuals Are Ladies

Sensitivity may appear to be a female characteristic; however, there are a number of men who are exceptionally sensitive. For some men, especially when sensitive, the notion of this being a myth that is true would be satisfying. However, the number of ladies that are sensitive are not higher than the percentage of men struggling with the same situation. As mentioned earlier in this book, men find their sense of masculinity stripped from them if they are classified as highly sensitive. But being a sensitive male does not mean your manliness isn't there anymore. It simply means that you think deeper about life in general – something your partner might really appreciate since you'd connect with them in a higher level than any other non-sensitive male would.

Being Sensitive Is a Negative Trait

Being exceptionally sensitive can feel more like a curse than a gift. However, the attribute accompanies numerous points of interest. HSPs can focus immensely, process material to more profound dimensions, adapt to new things without staying alert that they've learned, are better at learning dialects, have large amounts of sympathy and are regularly progressively heartfelt. The characteristic isn't an imperfection or a disorder. It's a benefit HSPs can figure out how to utilize and ensure.

In the Event That an Individual is Very Sensitive, They Don't Share it

Very sensitive individuals frequently conceal their quality out of dread of humiliation. To the outside spectator, they may seem to look and act like non-sensitive individuals, yet inside, they may feel on edge and overpowered.

Exceedingly Sensitive Individuals Decide Whether to Be Sensitive or Not

Exceedingly sensitive individuals are brought into the world with the attribute of affectability. Their sensory systems are entirely unique in relation to the sensory systems of non-sensitive individuals. This is an inborn attribute that individuals don't have a decision about, regardless of whether they have it or not.

It's Better Not to Be Exceptionally Sensitive

There's a drawback to being so sensitive, and there's a drawback to not being so sensitive. There's an upside to each; the two kinds of individuals have a ton of significant worth.

Exceptionally Sensitive Individuals Battle Having Relationships

Connections can be trying for very sensitive individuals; however, they're trying for non-sensitive individuals, as well. How profoundly sensitive individuals get hung up or hurt seeing someone is that they regularly look for the ideal or "extreme" relationship. Great connections take work, correspondence and mending from past injuries, regardless of whether the general population in the relationship are sensitive or not.

The Manner in Which an Exceedingly Sensitive Youngster Is Raised Doesn't Make a Difference

Sensitive youngsters must be brought up in situations that regard and oblige their tendencies. It's a logical actuality that sensitive kids brought up in great situations outflank non-sensitive kids scholastically and socially, yet sensitive kids brought up in terrible conditions are increasingly inclined to tension and wretchedness.

Exceptionally Sensitive Individuals Are Fundamentally the Same

The main things that we can say for sure that all exceptionally sensitive individuals share are the profundity of thought, overstimulation, passionate power, and tangible affectability. How somebody deals with those four things is so extraordinary unique to each individual.

Being Exceptionally Sensitive Is Equivalent to Being Candidly Powerless

Despite what might be expected, numerous very sensitive individuals are considered sincerely exceptional. Sensitive's power can be a blessing to the world, particularly when it's piped toward causes that they truly care about.

Chapter 20

When Is the Right Time to Seek Help If You Are an HSP?

As an HSP, you may have encountered circumstances and individuals who have left you doubting yourself, your observations, and your capacities. This is definitely not a positive sentiment and can leave you feeling defective somehow. We will, in general, stray from giving individuals access, dreading double-crossing, misfortune, or dismissal. It can feel hazardous for an HSP to request help, regardless of whether they feel tested and may battle at work, in their own lives or in their connections.

When we have injuries that need mending, for example, misuse or injury, it tends to overpower us, and we would need to trust somebody with our encounters to enable us to recuperate.

Below are a few tips for connecting and finding an advisor who will understand how to work with an exceptionally sensitive individual.

Beginning Your Inquiry

One of the principal proposals professionals make is to "value that this choice will profoundly affect your life." Acknowledge the choice, and set aside the opportunity to look into alternatives before choosing. Your specialist will be somebody you are letting into your life for a long time, reliably offering you a protected space to share encounters and proceed through testing feelings.

Finding an Authorized Advisor

Albeit numerous individuals offer administrations as a helping proficient, it is vital to search for advisors who have the correct instruction and licensure to rehearse in their field. Instances of this would be specialists, clinics, authorized advisors, and social laborers. There are state associations set up for these calling, and in spite of the fact that suppliers fluctuate extraordinarily, choosing somebody who is formally prepared and credentialed by their state board will enable you to realize that they have met the explicit criteria to rehearse in their field. Numerous advisors offer this data on their sites or different postings and if you can't find that data, don't be reluctant to get some information about their accreditations.

Where to Look

You can discover a great deal of data about specialists on the web. There are numerous internet postings and different sites committed to sharing data about accessible specialists and can be looked by area, so you can perceive what alternatives are accessible near you. Keep in mind that you will probably be seeing this individual for a while, so remember that as a top priority as you think about planning and driving.

A few specialists offer free face-to-face counsels or via telephone. If you discover an advisor who appears as though they would be a solid match for you, and they don't express that they offer a free interview, don't be hesitant to inquire. Most specialists will be happy to go through fifteen minutes via telephone, or even by email, to answer inquiries concerning their preparation and experience. Remember this conference time may be planned for development, and some may lean toward you come into the workplace for an in-person meeting.

Advisors inquire HSPs to try sharing enough data amid their interview or first session to accumulate data about how the specialist reacts in session. Interesting points may include:

- Is it accurate to say that they are receptive and occupied with the discussion?

- Do they appear to be humane and understanding?

- Do they enable you to share amid the primary session?

- Do you find that they have accommodating bits of knowledge?

- Do they enable you to make inquiries about their preparation or certifications?

Albeit a few advisors are very sensitive individuals themselves, others are most certainly not. It isn't really a prerequisite for your picked specialist to be an HSP like you, yet you may have that inclination. Enable yourself to accumulate the data important to know whether this is a sheltered domain and if the specialist understands the blessings and difficulties of HSPs.

Permit Yourself an opportunity to Choose

Subsequent to talking with a couple of advisors, set aside a little opportunity to leave and think about your alternatives. Think about things like their style and their office. It tends to be simple for exceptionally sensitive individuals to second guess themselves or questions their recognition. Keep in mind, you have an endowment of perusing prompts, so permit yourself an opportunity to think about the data you have assembled in your hunt, and settle on a strong choice of who may be the best fit for you.

Chapter 21

Inspirational Quotes for Sensitive Souls

"For a highly sensitive person, a drizzle feels like a monsoon."—Anonymous

"To feel intensely is not a symptom of weakness."

"Highly sensitive people are too often perceived as weaklings or damaged goods. To feel intensely is not a symptom of weakness, it is the trademark of the truly alive and compassionate. It is not the empath who is broken—it is the society that has become dysfunctional and emotionally disabled. There is no shame in expressing your authentic feelings. Those who are at times described as being a 'hot mess' or having 'too many issues' are the very fabric of what keeps the dream alive for a more caring, humane world. Never be ashamed to let your tears shine a light in this world."—Anthon St. Maarten, Divine Living: The Essential Guide to Your True Destiny

"Highly sensitive beings suffer more, but they also love harder."

"Dream wider and experience deeper horizons and bliss. When you're sensitive, you're alive in every sense of this word in this wildly beautiful world. Sensitivity is your strength. Keep soaking in the light and spreading it to others."—Victoria Erickson

"They hear nearly every sound, notice every movement, and process the expression on every person's face. And that means that simply walking through a public space can be an assault on their senses."—Andre Sólo, Everything You Need to Know about Highly Sensitive People

"We try to be like others. But that leads to our becoming over-aroused and distressed."

"We are a package deal, however. Our trait of sensitivity means we will also be cautious, inward, needing extra time alone. Because people without the trait (the majority) do not understand that, they see us as timid, shy, weak, or that greatest sin of all, unsociable. Fearing these labels, we try to be like others. But that leads to our becoming over-aroused and distressed. Then that gets us labeled neurotic or crazy, first by others and then by ourselves."—Elaine N. Aron, The Highly Sensitive Person: How to Thrive When the World Overwhelms You

"No matter who it is or how comfortable you are with someone, when anyone yells at you or talks down to you, you immediately erupt in tears."—Lauren Jarvis-Gibson, 11 Things People Don't Realize You're Doing Because You're a Highly Sensitive Person

"As a highly sensitive person, I can sense your mood from a mile away. Don't try to hide it. You're not fooling me."—Tracy M. Kusmierz, 9 Things I Wish People Knew about Me as a Highly Sensitive Introvert

"Am I too sensitive to be in this world?"

"How do you ever explain the feelings of anxiety and paralyzing fear? I can't answer those questions. It's just a feeling of 'Am I crazy? Am I too sensitive to be in this world?' A feeling that the world is just too complicated for me right now, and I don't feel like I belong here. But it passes, and fortunately today I feel blessed for all the good things in my life."—Winona Ryder

"I'm extremely-extremely sensitive. I can cry at the drop of a hat. Anything upsets me. I cry all the time. I cry when I'm happy too."—Mandy Moore

10. "Sensitive people like a slower pace of life. We like pondering all our options before making a decision and regularly reflecting on our experiences. We hate busy schedules and rushing from one event to the next."—Jenn Granneman, 12 Things a Highly Sensitive Person Needs

"As a highly sensitive person, every little thing elicits a strong reaction in me."—Tracy M. Kusmierz, 9 Things I Wish People Knew about Me as a Highly Sensitive Introvert

"Being a sensitive empath is a beautiful thing as an artist."

"I am very sensitive to the interactions I have with people. Whether it's a momentary glance in an elevator, or a deep philosophical conversation over dinner, or a brush-by in a café, I feel (sometimes exhaustingly) attuned and affected by the subtle exchanges that pass seemingly benignly between us as human ships. Being a sensitive empath is a beautiful thing as an artist, and it fosters a deep burning curiosity about why we do the things we do."—Alanis Morissette

"You desperately want to be understood."—Marisa Donnelly, 10 Ways Women Raised by Sensitive Fathers Love Differently

"There is nothing wrong with you if there are times you get weighed down by the heaviness of the suffering in the world."—Rachel Samson

"By some strange, unknown, inward urgency they are not really alive unless they are creating."

"The truly creative mind in any field is no more than this: A human creature born abnormally, inhumanly sensitive. To them a touch is a blow, a sound is a noise, a misfortune is a tragedy, a joy is an ecstasy, a friend is a lover, a lover is a god, and failure is death. Add to this cruelly delicate organism the overpowering necessity to create, create, create—so that without the creating of music or poetry or books or buildings or something of meaning, their very breath is cut off. They must create, must pour out creation. By some strange, unknown, inward urgency they are not really alive unless they are creating."—Pearl Buck, The Good Earth

"Highly sensitive people learned early in life to try to control the external world as a way to attempt to manage their inner one."—Sheryl Paul

"Everything I experience hits me deep, raw, and intense. As an empath, I feel the energy of myself and others. As I age, this ability only grows deeper and stranger."—Sylvester McNutt III

"Even a moderate and familiar stimulation like a day at work can cause a highly sensitive person to need quiet by evening."—Elaine N. Aron, The Highly Sensitive Person: How to Thrive When the World Overwhelms You

"Highly sensitive people tend to have stronger emotional responses than others."

"Partly, this is because they notice so many emotional cues that others miss, so they're very 'tuned in' to feelings. But it's also because HSPs process things so deeply. Imagine if you felt every emotion five times longer and five times louder; that's kind of what it's like to be an HSP."—Andre Sólo, How to Explain High Sensitivity to People Who Don't "Get" It

"I can't stand chaos. I hate loud environments. Art makes me cry. No, I'm not crazy; I'm a textbook example of a highly sensitive person."—Anne Marie Crosthwaite, You're Not Crazy, You're a Highly Sensitive Person

"The real warriors in this world are the ones that see the details of another's soul."

"They see the transparency behind walls people put up. They stand on the battlefield of life and expose their heart's transparency, so others can finish the day with hope. They are the sensitive souls that understand that before they could be a light, they first had to feel the burn."—Shannon L. Alder

"It seems my heart is made of tissue paper; I wish the world would handle it more delicately."—Richelle E. Goodrich

"Being highly sensitive is both a gift and a responsibility."

"Learning to thrive as a highly sensitive soul presents challenges. If you're sensitive, you have likely accumulated years of training in trying to overcome the trait because you don't 'fit in' with society. And yet being highly sensitive is a vital part of you. A first step toward thriving as a sensitive soul is to understand and accept your trait. Hear this now: There is absolutely nothing wrong with you. You are just different. As one of my clients says, being highly sensitive is both a gift and a responsibility."—HSP life coach Jenna Avery

"The highly sensitive person has an important mission."

"The highly sensitive person has an important mission, which is to serve as a balance to the more aggressive behavior of some of the non-HSPs who advocate a less than nurturing policy toward humans, animals, and Mother Nature."—Ted Zeff, The Highly Sensitive Person's Survival Guide: Essential Skills for Living Well in an Overstimulating World

"By noticing and processing so many details around them—not to mention their own internal thoughts—highly sensitive people are doing far more cognitive work than most others. Being overstimulated and frazzled is something anyone can identify with, but for HSPs, it happens much more easily."—Andre Sólo

"One of my favorite aspects of high sensitivity is finding wonder in the smallest of things."—Cati Vanden Breul, 8 Reasons Being Highly Sensitive Is Actually a Good Thing

"High sensitivity is not a disease or a disorder. It's not something that needs to be overcome or fixed."—Jenn Granneman

"I don't think there's any artist of any value who doesn't doubt what they're doing." – Francis Ford Coppola

"A creative man is motivated by the desire to achieve, not by the desire to beat others." – Ayn Rand

"Creativity is just connecting things. When you ask creative people how they did something, they feel a little guilty because they didn't really do it, they just saw something. It seemed obvious to them after a while. That's because they were able to connect experiences they've had and synthesize new things." – Steve Jobs

"I think an artist's responsibility is more complex than people realize." – Jodie Foster

"Always do your best. What you plant now, you will harvest later." – Og Mandino

"Imagination is more important than knowledge." – Albert Einstein

"An essential aspect of creativity is not being afraid to fail." – Edwin Land

"Clean out a corner of your mind and creativity will instantly fill it." – Dee Hock

"Art is the most intense mode of individualism that the world has known." – Oscar Wilde

"Even a true artist does not always produce art." – Carroll O'Connor

"Creativity can be described as letting go of certainties." – Gail Sheehy

"An artist cannot fail; it is a success to be one." – Charles Horton Cooley

"The weeds keep multiplying in our garden, which is our mind ruled by fear. Rip them out and call them by name." – Sylvia Browne

"An artist is not paid for his labor but for his vision." – James Whistler

"Can you imagine what I would do if I could do all I can?" – Sun Tzu

"I like nonsense, it wakes up the brain cells. Fantasy is a necessary ingredient in living, it's a way of looking at life through the wrong end of a telescope. Which is what I do, and that enables you to laugh at life's realities." – Dr. Seuss

"Imagination will often carry us to worlds that never were. But without it we go nowhere." – Carl Sagan

"The imagination is man's power over nature." – Wallace Stevens

"Believe in yourself! Have faith in your abilities! Without a humble but reasonable confidence in your own powers you cannot be successful or happy." – Norman Vincent Peale

"Do you want to know who you are? Don't ask. Act! Action will delineate and define you." – Thomas Jefferson

"If you don't design your own life plan, chances are you'll fall into someone else's plan. And guess what they have planned for you? Not much." – Jim Rohn

"If you've got a talent, protect it." – Jim Carrey

"Live out of your imagination, not your history." – Stephen Covey

"It's always too early to quit." – Norman Vincent Peale

"Small deeds done are better than great deeds planned." – Peter Marshall

Conclusion

To close off on the delicate being of the sensitive soul, Elena Herdieckerhoff (1) provides, in her inspirational speech, a way for all sensitives to come together and thrive:

Highly sensitive person, what's the first thing you think about when I tell you that there must be shy and introverted or perhaps very emotional? Or maybe even that you need to walk on eggshells around me?

The common assumption about highly sensitive people is that we are somehow weak and fragile creatures that pick a losing ticket in the genetic lottery of life.

You can see this in action. When you Google the word sensitive you will see images of too thick irritated skin, wilted dandelions, and crying people.

Sensitivity clearly has a PR problem, and today I want to help change that. Maybe by now you're wondering what it is like to be highly sensitive.

I invite you to imagine living with all of your senses on high alert. You also have a vivid in a world where all of your emotions are magnified. Sadness is deep sorrow, and joy is pure ecstasy. He also cares beyond reason and empathizes without limits.

Imagine being impermanent, in a small say with everything around you being highly sensitive. People often hear things like, "You are too sensitive," "Stop taking everything to heart or my favorite," "You should really toughen up."

The fundamental message is clear. To be highly sensitive is to be highly flawed. I used to agree with that I was—thought I should come with some sort of warning sign or disclaimer.

Now, let me share with you a few of the perks of being a highly sensitive person. For one, I have an intensely overactive mind, which means it's impossible to switch off. That also means that insomnia is my best friend. As you can imagine, that comes in particularly handy the night before a talk.

Also, I cannot watch scary or violent movies because the images seem to haunt me forever. I remember when I was a child I watched the movie Jaws it traumatized me so much that I was unable to even go near a swimming pool let alone the sea for several years and embarrassingly enough, I do my childhood nickname of "Princess on the Pea" proud when it comes to traveling and hotels.

Everything should be not too hard, not too soft. It has to be just right. It was recommended that I should simply start traveling with my own bed and pillow when traveling.

I often wondered, what good could it possibly do me to be this way? Well, the gifts of sensitivity slowly crept up on me. I've come to learn to love that I deeply easily connect with others, and also that I have a strong intuition that guides me like an infallible GPS.

It is said that highly sensitive people are people who have a genetic trait of sensory processing sensitivity. That's quite a mouthful. And, surprisingly, 15 to 20 percent of the population is highly sensitive.

As species, we have a phenomenal ability to deeply analyze absolutely everything. My favorite example of this is what I like to call Chinese restaurant syndrome. Basically, we can take up to an hour to read the entire forty-page menu despite the fact that we'll very likely order our favorite dish anyway.

We get quickly overwhelmed by the world around us. I, for one, love going to carnivals but I actually have to leave after an hour because I get completely overpowered by the mix of roast chicken smells—with candy floss and the cacophony of songs and the massive crowds. It is too much for my senses.

Sensitive individuals constantly experience empathy and feel what others feel. It's like that old Hebrew saying when one cries the other tests salt.

With that said, sensitive individuals can pick up on sounds others may not be aware of. Unfortunately, it means that they're also the kind of people that will wake you up at 3:00 a.m. to tell you that there is tapping in the kitchen two floors down.

As you can see, being a sensitive is about far more than emotional reactivity. I would like to address the two big elephants in the room when it comes to a highly sensitive stereotype. The first assumption is that these individuals must simply be undercover introverts that wanted offense.

The fact of the matter is 30 percent of sensitives are actually extroverts, which means we cannot park them in the convenient quite wallflower category.

Another stereotype, I found, is because of the supposed conclusion that femininity of a sensitive's traits many assume that these individuals are women, may come a surprise that 50 percent of them are in fact men.

Men are not supposed to be sensitive but aggressive and have compassion. Sadly, the notion that men can be both sensitive and strong is still too much of an alien concept.

Now it is a good time to tell you that I don't think one is better or worse than the other. They are simply different. I would also like to point out, despite the rumors that they are not members of the special snowflake society or have a secret handshake to identify each other, sensitives are like everyone else except that they experience the world in a more vivid way. And if you think that all agencies are alike, that's not true. Every sensitive has their own unique sensitive fingerprint alongside other identity markers like gender, ethnicity, and cultural and personal background,

I would also like to point out that being a sensitive is not an illness and it is also not a choice. It is a genetic trait. We are essentially born to be mild. Every time you tell a sensitive they are too sensitive, it's like telling someone who has blue eyes that their eyes are too blue.

Chances are no matter how often you tell them, you will still have the same blue eyes looking back at you as a society. We have come to think of sensitivity as a flaw and unfortunate emotional circumstances that temper our ability to become ever more optimized, detached and robotic. We all readily belittle the idea.

Sensitives are dreamers and creators. This was, however, not always the case. In previous centuries, philanthropists, philosophers, poets, artists, and painters were all venerated for their sensitive contribution to society.

Who would we be without Leonardo da Vinci? Or without a Mozart, or Balzac, or Mother Teresa, or Ghandi? I would most certainly be a shade darker.

Now, I'm not suggesting that all sensitives are geniuses that shape the world. But most sensitives have a genuine urge to create a connection and meaning. Because they feel every pain they see. They want to elevate the forgotten and save the misfortunate when they are at peace trying to hide.

With their sensitivity to fit in, we all lose what a poor society lacks; the beating heart of sensitive creation that discredits imagination, intuition, and empathy.

That is why we need to urgently start to accept and appreciate sensitivity for the temperature regulating effect it has on an often hot-headed world.

I believe we're all sensitive to different degrees, and in different ways, it is peace or simply at the far end of the spectrum. That is why how we think in talking about sensitivity concerns all of us. We need to come together as a society to rewrite the negative cultural narrative about sensitivity and turn it into a positive one. We need to embrace the notion that sensitivity is a weakness to finally benefit from its many strengths.

By doing so, we create an environment where everybody is safe to express their softer side, not just a chess piece. How can we go about creating more positive awareness and acceptance for sensitivity on a public level? I believe the two most urgent changes need to happen in schools and in the workplace.

In schools, we need to train our teachers to recognize and understand sensitive children and for parents and teachers alike. They often desire to toughen them up to survive in the big world that their needs to stop. We should not try to force sheep into Wolf's clothing on a corporate level. The system is set up to favor those with steel elbows because sensitive people typically are more soft-spoken and cooperative. Instead of competitive, they often get left behind on the corporate ladder.

137

To change this, we need to create an environment where all personality types can flourish, and not just a select few. That is why I believe for corporations. It is in their own best interest to invite sensitive people to the table because without sensitive they risk lacking innovation, integrity, and ultimately, humanity.

On a personal level, we can all make an impact simply by refraining from judging the delicate difference of the sensitives around us. The next time you feel like telling someone, "You're too sensitive," I would ask you to stop and pause and fill that pause with us.

Understanding, you will see that the simple act of acceptance will uplift both of you to my fellow edges. Take heart and be unashamedly yourself. Stop trying to toughen up. Stop hiding your beautiful as you are.

Don't feel weird because it's not you who can be considered wrong, but rather a world in which corruption and violence in greed are the norm. It's no measure of health to be well adjusted to a profoundly sick society.

When I was a little girl, I loved chasing butterflies in our garden, and I admired their fragile beauty. I felt a deep urge to protect them, so I decided to trap them in little mason jars filled with grass and flowers. To keep them safe with me in my room. I quickly understood butterflies did not like captivity.

This made me understand they did not need to be rescued. Their colorful contribution to the natural ecosystem was exactly as it should be. Similarly, sensitives should not hide away from the pain of this world in a protective incubator is their role to step up and share their sensitive gifts with all of us.

I believe as humans we are all united by our experience of sensitivity and empathy.

Also, I don't believe you need to be sensitive to care and to make a difference. We are facing grave political, cultural and environmental problems today. Now more than ever.

We need the contribution of sensitive minds and hearts to pave a path for the troubled times ahead. The more we all allow ourselves to connect to our innate sensitive gifts. The more we can heal ourselves and the planet we live on.

Resources

Aron, E. Self-Tests—The Highly Sensitive Person. Hsperson.com. Available at: https://hsperson.com/test/

Chernoff, A. 10 Life-Changing Tips for Highly Sensitive People. Marc and Angel Hack Life. Available at: http://www.marcandangel.com/2015/07/22/10-life-changing-tips-for-highly-sensitive-people/

Eby, S. Highly Sensitive People and Depression. Highly Sensitive and Creative. Available at: http://highlysensitive.org/highly-sensitive-people-and-depression-overstimulation-may-lead-to-depression/

Focus on the Family. Understanding Highly Sensitive Children. Available at: https://www.focusonthefamily.ca/content/understanding-highly-sensitive-children

Granneman, J. 11 Myths *about Being Highly Sensitive*. IntrovertDear.com. Available at: https://introvertdear.com/news/myths-about-being-highly-sensitive/

Granneman, J. 14 Things Highly Sensitive People Absolutely Need to Be Happy. Highly Sensitive Refuge. Available at: https://highlysensitiverefuge.com/things-highly-sensitive-people-need-happy/

Granneman, J. 17 Way-Too-Personal Confessions of an Introvert. IntrovertDear.com. Available at: https://introvertdear.com/news/introvert-confessions-personal/

Greene, L. Why Is Pet Loss Especially Hard for Highly Sensitive People? Highly Sensitive Refuge. Available at: https://highlysensitiverefuge.com/losing-pet-highly-sensitive-people/

Highly Sensitive Refuge. What Is a Highly Sensitive Person? (A Relatable Guide) | Highly Sensitive Refuge. Available at: https://highlysensitiverefuge.com/what-is-highly-sensitive-person/485/

Psychology Today. 24 Signs of a Highly Sensitive Person. Available at: https://www.psychologytoday.com/us/blog/communication-success/201711/24-signs-highly-sensitive-person

Psychology Today. Are You Highly Sensitive and Bipolar? Available at: https://www.psychologytoday.com/us/blog/sense-and-sensitivity/201707/are-you-highly-sensitive-and-bipolar

Stuckey, Q. The Double Whammy of Being a Highly Sensitive Man. Highly Sensitive Refuge. Available at: https://highlysensitiverefuge.com/highly-sensitive-man-whammy/

Sólo, A. The 7 Best Careers for a Highly Sensitive Person. Highly Sensitive Refuge. Available at: https://highlysensitiverefuge.com/highly-sensitive-person-careers/

Sólo, A. The Difference between a Highly Sensitive Brain and a "Typical" Brain. Highly Sensitive Refuge. Available at: https://highlysensitiverefuge.com/highly-sensitive-person-brain/

Sólo, A. What Happens When a Highly Sensitive Person Grows Up with Emotional Neglect? Highly Sensitive Refuge. Available at: https://highlysensitiverefuge.com/childhood-emotional-neglect/ Sólo, A. (2019). Why Travel Is Hard for Highly Sensitive People (and How to Enjoy It More). Highly Sensitive Refuge. Available at: https://highlysensitiverefuge.com/highly-sensitive-person-travel/

"The Gentle Power of Highly Sensitive People." Elena Herdieckerhoff. Available at https://www.youtube.com/watch?v=pi4JOlMSWjo (1)

The Healthy Sensitive. 12 Tricks to Help Highly Sensitive People Develop a Balanced Workout Plan They Actually Like. Available at: https://thehealthysensitive.com/2018/05/16/12-tricks-to-help-highly-sensitive-people-develop-a-balanced-workout-plan-they-actually-like/

Thought Catalog. 21 Ways to Take Care of a Highly Sensitive Person. Available at: https://thoughtcatalog.com/sophia-borghese/2015/02/21-ways-to-take-care-of-a-highly-sensitive-person/

Trittin, L. Why Do Highly Sensitive People Absorb Other People's Emotions? Highly Sensitive Refuge. Available at: https://highlysensitiverefuge.com/highly-sensitive-people-absorb-emotions/

Verywell Mind. Finding the Right Therapist as a Highly Sensitive Person. Available at: https://www.verywellmind.com/finding-a-therapist-as-a-highly-sensitive-person-4159535

Winter, C. 12 Things Highly Sensitive People Notice That Most Others Don't. A Conscious Rethink. Available at: https://www.aconsciousrethink.com/6104/things-highly-sensitive-people-notice/

Made in the USA
Lexington, KY
07 April 2019